IMAGES *of our Past*

HISTORIC BLACK NOVA SCOTIA

BRIDGLAL PACHAI & HENRY BISHOP

NIMBUS
PUBLISHING

The authors salute
the pioneering African Nova Scotians
whose legacy exemplifies
dignity, devotion, and determination.

Nimbus Publishing Limited
PO Box 9166
Halifax, NS B3K 5M8
(902) 455-4286
www.nimbus.ns.ca

Printed and bound in Canada
Interior design: Kathy Kaulbach, Touchstone Design.

Front cover: Children at the Stairs Street School. It ceased operation as a segregated school in 1915 and was closed in 1924.

Title page: Loyal Wilberforce Lodge, No. 7336, I.O.O.F., Halifax, Nova Scotia, 1917. Seated front row centre is C. H. Johnston. Back row, eighth from left is Rev. W. N. States.

Library and Archives Canada Cataloguing in Publication

Pachai, Bridglal
Historic Black Nova Scotia / Bridglal Pachai and Henry Bishop.
Includes bibliographical references.
ISBN 1-55109-551-3

1. Black Canadians—Nova Scotia—History. I. Bishop, Henry II. Title.

FC2350.B6P34 2006   971.6004'96   C2006-900741-1

Canada

The Canada Council | Le Conseil des Arts
for the Arts | du Canada

We acknowledge the financial support of the Government of Canada through the Book Publishing Industry Development Program (BPIDP) and the Canada Council, and of the Province of Nova Scotia through the Department of Tourism, Culture and Heritage for our publishing activities.

Contents

Acknowledgments

In a work of illustrated history, much depends on the availability of photographs. Over a twenty-year period we have been fortunate to come across quite a number. Through our travels and researches in Nova Scotia we have met many resourceful individuals whose help we could count upon. We give thanks to these many, some listed here.

The Public Archives of Nova Scotia and the Black Cultural Centre are two repositories that stand out. Their cooperation and resources have served us well. The Dalhousie University Archives and senior archivist Dr. Kathryn Harvey have been most cooperative, as have the Black Loyalist Society and its president, Elizabeth Cromwell; the Black Business Initiative and its executive director, Rustum Southwell; the Nova Scotia Advisory Council on the Status of Women and its executive director, Brigitte Neumann; the Nova Scotia Home for Coloured Children and its executive director, Wilfred Jackson; Joey Patterson; the Hantsport Historical Society; and Queen's University Archives.

The following individuals deserve special mention for their cooperation and help: Graham Downey, Kenneth Crawford, Eugene Williams, Irvine Carvery, Joyce Ruck De Peza, Barry Cahill, Philip Hartling, Beverly Bonvie, Orval and Geraldine Browning, Dr. Leslie Oliver, Mayann Francis, David States, Rev. Sherrolyn Riley, Rev. Donald Fairfax, Rev. Willard Clayton and Mrs. Jean Clayton, Sylvia Bell and Winnie Milne, Dr. Lorne White, Dr. Wayne Adams, Dr. Carolyn Thomas, Laura Daye, George Borden, Arthur Ruck, Mrs. Joyce Calvin Ruck, Dr. Vincent Audain, Dr. Renn Holness, and Archbishop Vincent M. Waterman.

The team at Nimbus Publishing—Dan Soucoup, Sandra McIntyre, and staff—have been very helpful and cordial. The editorial comments and suggestions by Zsofi Koller and Robert Plowman have contributed to improvements in the contents and structure of the book. Finally, our sincere thanks to Chauna James for conscientious typing of an earlier version of the text.

Bridglal Pachai and Henry Bishop

Authors' Note

A frican Nova Scotians are one of the four charter peoples of Nova
Scotia whose presence and contribution range from the seventeenth
century to the twenty-first century. Alongside the Aboriginal peoples,
the Acadians, and the British, the story of African Nova Scotians is the story
of their arrival, settlement, dispersion, adjustment, trials and tribulations,
and their contribution to family, community, colony, province, and nation.
In the period of over four hundred years they have been referred to variously
as Africans, Negroes, coloureds, blacks, African Nova Scotians, and African
Canadians.

Writing this book is an opportunity to engage in a dialogue between the past
and the present through the minds of the present. It is only the present that
can keep the past alive through its curiosities, its questions, its interests, and its
debates.

This is not a comprehensive history. The assignment which the authors have
undertaken is to tell a story, mainly of the distant past, through selected images.
One of the authors has spent a lifetime in many continents, mainly Africa, teaching and writing about both sides of the diasporic experience. The other has spent
his entire lifetime in the province of Nova Scotia, knows the travails of being
black in this province and country, but knows also how to break barriers, work
on images as a graphic artist, and educate through illustrations, presentations,
and music. For over twenty years they have collaborated in different ways and
places on the subject of the African Nova Scotian experience, such as the celebration of Black Boxers Reunion and the exhibition and publication of *Africville: A
Spirit that Lives On.*

They share a common interest in human advancement through education.
At times together, and many times separately, they have taken the story of the
African Nova Scotian experience into classrooms and university lecture rooms,
making presentations locally, regionally, nationally, and internationally. Both
have produced other publications separately over the years and now welcome this
opportunity to present their major joint effort, twenty years after they worked
as colleagues during the foundation years of the Black Cultural Centre for Nova
Scotia.

The story of black settlements and black pioneers, of obstacles and organizations, of initiatives and achievements, of failures and frustrations, is a fascinating
story that is the subject of this volume. Previous pioneering studies of aspects of

the African Nova Scotian experience by Robin Winks, James Walker, and John Grant, among the notable few, were buttressed by valuable contributions by organizations like the Black Educators Association and the Black Cultural Centre for Nova Scotia. African Nova Scotian poets like Maxine Tynes, George Elliott Clarke, and George Borden have recaptured and reinforced the black experience in powerful verse while playwrights like Walter Borden and George Boyd have put on centre stage the power and the personalities of the African diaspora. Selections from these contributions are presented in the chapters that follow.

The authors recognize that any volume, whose main focus is to trace the legacy of the past through the medium of illustrated texts, depends largely on the availability of suitable photographs. When this exercise deals with an entire province—in this case, Nova Scotia—an added constraint is the need for fair representation. Within these guidelines of available illustrations and province-wide representation, the authors have attempted to highlight selected themes of the Nova Scotia black experience: immigration and settlement; the Baptist Church and its institutions and personalities, early publications advocating black aspirations and achievements, the legal profession and practitioners who served the black community, early publishers who provided a medium to share experiences, secular organizations that complemented the work and programs of the Black Baptist Church, and role models drawn from various sectors of black society. The inclusion of a postscript on the Africville experience serves as a reminder of the persistence of a common expression in the annals of the African Nova Scotian story, now in its fifth century, namely, the struggle continues.

Introduction

Nova Scotia occupies a special place in the story of the African diaspora in Eastern Canada. It was the main home of the first arrivals between the seventeenth and nineteenth centuries in four identifiable groups: slaves, Black Loyalists, Maroons, and Black Refugees. There were individuals, too, like the sailor/interpreter Mathieu DaCosta and the entrepreneur/land-owner Barbara Cuffy, who cannot be slotted into any group. These groups, and their descendants, were joined in the next two centuries by individuals and families of the African diaspora from countries all over the world. Today, members of this diaspora have evolved beyond group identities into Canadian nation builders.

Canadians of African descent number almost 700,000 in 2005. When com-bined with the population of Africa and persons of African descent living all over the world, a total figure of almost half a billion emerges. In an age of interdepen-dence such a figure is of significance.

Yet for so very long, people of the African continent as well as of the African diaspora have had to endure considerable hardships inflicted by the institutions of slavery, colonialism, imperialism, and exploitation. The story of the African presence in Nova Scotia is no exception to this generality, even if the scale was smaller than elsewhere as a result of numbers, geography, and changing social and economic factors.

The first recorded information of the African presence on Nova Scotian soil is that of the seaman Mathieu Da Costa, a member of the French expedition that landed at Port Royal in 1605. Da Costa is credited with having knowledge of the Mi'kmaq language, a fact that suggests previous contact and also draws attention to a well-known feature in African societies: the ability to master many tongues. Before Da Costa's century ran out, it was recorded that, in 1686, a black person was living on Cape Sable Island.

Twenty-three years after Da Costa's arrival, slavery was reported in Quebec. It was confirmed as a practice in British Canada in 1660. Thus, as European immigrants arrived in Nova Scotia in later years, either from Europe or from other parts of North America, they brought their slaves with them as domestic labourers in small numbers. The largest single importation of slaves came to the Maritimes in 1783–84 with their Loyalist masters. Of the total number of 1,232 slaves brought to the Maritimes during these years, Nova Scotia accounted for 1,194. However, the absence of a plantation economy and the opposition of the

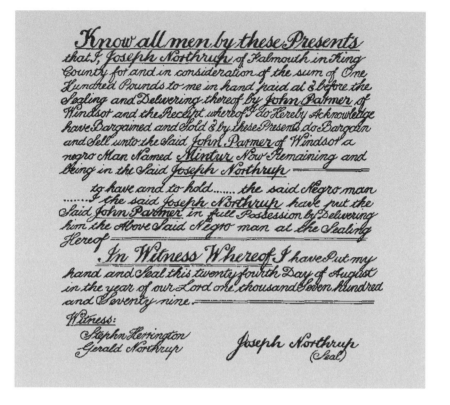

Know all men by these Presents that I, Joseph Northrup of Falmouth in King County for and in consideration of the sum of One Hundred Pounds to me in hand paid at & before the Sealing and Delivering thereof by John Parmer of Windsor and the Receipt whereof I do Hereby Acknowledge have Bargained and Sold & by these Presents do Bargain and Sell unto the said John Parmer of Windsor a negro Man Named Minter Now Remaining and Being in the Said Joseph Northrup

to have and to hold....... the said Negro man .... I the said Joseph Northrup have put the said John Parmer in full Possession by Delivering him the Above said Negro man at the Sealing Hereof

In Witness Whereof I have Put my hand and Seal this twenty fourth Day of August in the year of our Lord one thousand Seven Hundred and Seventy nine.

Witness:
Stephn Herrington
Gerald Northrup

Joseph Northrup
(Seal)

law courts combined to discourage the practice of slavery. Decades before the emancipation of slaves in the British empire in 1834, slavery had ceased to exist in Nova Scotia.

When Halifax was founded in 1749, there were persons of African descent in the town. These comprised both free and enslaved persons. In one case it was reported that some fifteen black persons were issued with rations in 1750 in Halifax. Since slaves were the responsibility of their owners, recipients of rations were free persons in dire need. In 1760, when the Nova Scotia government opened up new lands to immigrants, free blacks came from the New England colonies to stake their claims in parts of Nova Scotia. One of them, Barbara Cuffy, was one of the founders of the town of Liverpool in her capacity as a principal shareholder.

Blacks were relatively numerous in Nova Scotia at this time. In the census of 1767, Nova Scotia's population was 13,374. The leading immigrant ethnic groups were the Irish with 853 and the English with 302. Blacks numbered 104 while the Scots, whose numbers increased in later years, numbered just 52.

The greatest influx into Nova Scotia of members of the African diaspora took place when the Black Loyalists were brought to the province by the British government during and after the American War of Independence. Between 1782 and 1784 some 3,500 free Black Loyalists settled in Nova Scotia, and in 1784 a few of this number went to New Brunswick. The black population rose to 10 per cent of Nova Scotia's total population—the largest it has ever been in the history of Nova Scotia. This proportion was reduced when one-third left to return permanently to their ancestral home in Africa in 1792, due to a number of factors, including settlement in unsuitable farming areas, considerable delays in land grants, long distances from employment areas, harsh weather conditions, and unsympathetic government officials. This emigration of some 1,196 persons included the preachers and teachers of the time, the leaders and the landowners, the skilled and the free. Africa gained from David George, Thomas Peters, Joseph Leonard, Adam and Catherine Abernathy, Moses Wilkinson, and Boston King, distinguished emigrants whose experience in Nova Scotia represented a sore point in the treatment accorded to British subjects of African descent.

The proportion of blacks in Nova Scotia's population was never the same after 1792, even though two major immigrant groups arrived not long afterwards: the Maroons from Jamaica and the Black Refugees from the United States.

As for the first of these, the Maroons, some 511 arrived in the province in 1796 and some 550 left the country permanently in 1800. The temporary sojourn of the Maroons was part of a colonial design to quell the spirit of a rebellious people who were proud of their freedom and their cohesiveness. Of all the members of the African diaspora who set foot on Nova Scotian soil, the Maroons were the only ones who did not look to Canada as the land of promise and plenty, of safety and security, of freedom and fortune. All these the Maroons had already sought and fought for in their native land. They were caught up in a colonial conflict in Jamaica and in Nova Scotia. In Jamaica, their militancy was a threat; in Nova Scotia, their stubbornness and refusal to toe the official line were deemed to be a threat to a conservative white society not accustomed to black assertiveness. And so, they too had to move on.

The Black Refugees came as a result of British support and promises during the war that broke out between Britain and the United States in 1812. They arrived in Nova Scotia between 1813 and 1816, adding some two thousand persons to the population. These refugees came from the southern states where they were still in bondage. The history of their arrival and settlement makes for a fascinating story: they were invited and encouraged to come, but no prior arrangements were made to receive them, to settle them, or to make them welcome additions to an expanding province. In desperation, the governor of the day, Sir John Coape Sherbrooke, placed them in a poor house in Halifax and on Melville Island, once a stronghold for prisoners, off the Halifax North West Arm. Only later were they settled in various communities in and around Halifax.

By this time, persons of African descent had been in and out of Nova Scotia for some two hundred years, but their position was still precarious. In February 1815, the governor informed the House of Assembly that the black refugees entering the province were providing much needed labour in agriculture, in spite of the difficult circumstances under which they arrived. Governor Sherbrooke asked that they be given government grants, including land grants, to enable them to make a good beginning with their new lives. The members of the House ignored this request. Instead, two months later, in April 1815, they attacked the "character, principles and habits" of the new black immigrants, claiming that the majority of them competed unfairly with white labourers and servants, being unfitted by nature to live in the Canadian climate or to associate with the white colonists. The House requested that black immigrants be prohibited from entering Nova Scotia.

Had it not been for international commitments by the British House of Commons to promote a humanitarian movement everywhere in the British empire, not only would black immigration to Nova Scotia have been prohibited in the early decades of the nineteenth century, but blacks likely would have been deported from Nova Scotia in the next few years, if the mood and the motions of the legislative assembly were anything to go by.

From 1816 onwards, the reality was that members of the African diaspora were in Nova Scotia to stay; segregated black settlements sprang up in various places, including Preston, Hamonds Plains, Beech Hill, Cobequid Road, Windsor Road, Africville, Birchtown, Digby, and Guysborough. Inducements surfaced from time to time to encourage them to relocate to other parts of the British Empire. Except for ninety-five persons who elected to go to Trinidad in 1821, the black population of Nova Scotia was determined to stay on, for better or for worse. In the census of 1851, the number of black men was recorded as 2,321 and the number of black women as 2,587, giving a total of 4,908. (The number of children was not recorded.) More than a century later, in 1964, Rev. W. P. Oliver surveyed the forty-seven black communities that then existed in Nova Scotia, and arrived at a total black population of 14,000, of which the largest was North Preston (1,800), followed by Halifax (1,300).

The rest of the story provides ample evidence of the themes that had taken root in the early years. Organizations and institutions were put in place to give expression to the African voice in Nova Scotia. For the remainder of the nineteenth century, it was the African United Baptist Association, founded in 1854, which bore the burden of this role. The Baptist church became the cement of the family and the pillar for the community. The first distinguished church leader of the nineteenth century, Richard Preston, who provided leadership from 1816 to 1861 and in the process established a Mutual Aid Improvement Society and an Anti-Slavery Society, was but the first in a long line of distinguished Baptist leaders, which included Wellington States, William Andrew White, William Pearly Oliver, Donald Fairfax, and Donald Skeir.

In the course of time, and up to World War II, the African voice and African aspirations were echoed by other organizations, including the Halifax Colored Citizens Improvement League founded by Beresford Augustus Husbands in 1932 (and headed by him for thirty-six years) and the Colored Education Centre founded by the Guyanese physician Dr. F. Holder in 1938.

As in Africa, the tempo of the activities increased in the period following the Atlantic Charter in 1941 and the end of the war in 1945. While the previous incipient nationalist movements in Africa developed into lively mass-nationalist movements after 1945, culminating in independence for the colonies, in Nova Scotia the period was marked by the emergence of a number of secular organizations that extended the scope of political participation and increased the demands for improvements in housing, employment, education, and human rights. Though the political process was nothing like the civil rights movement in the United States, the new organizations worked hard to bring about meaningful changes in a society in which race relations were based upon the well-laid foundations of white superiority and dominance. Inroads were hard to make and changes were slow in coming.

BLACK PIONEERS MAKING THEIR WAY ALONG A ROAD NEAR HALIFAX, AS PAINTED BY ROBERT PETLEY, C.1835

The Nova Scotia Association for the Advancement of Coloured People was formed in 1945 and continued to exist for over fifty years. At a time when it was the only provincial body to articulate the concerns of the black population, its work was invaluable. Through its efforts new areas of employment opened up and instances of racial discrimination were brought to the attention of the courts and the public. When Nova Scotia passed the Fair Employment Practices Act in 1955 and the Fair Accommodations Act in 1959, the influence and the impact of NSAACP were evident. It was only in the late 1960s that other organizations appeared on the scene.

The factors and circumstances that led to the formation of the Black United Front are traceable to the changing order in the 1960s on the international, continental, and national scenes. Nova Scotia's black population felt the surge of independence movements in Africa, civil rights movements in the United States, and events on the Canadian scene relating to biculturalism and bilingualism, and ultimately to multiculturalism. There were emerging precedents for action that could bring about changes, including strikes, boycotts, dialogue, coalitions, and cooperation. Older people influenced by years of experience rubbed shoulders with younger people with urgency and militancy in their minds and on their agendas. It was a time for change, for a meeting of minds, for an amalgam for united actions. From this exciting mix, the Black United Front was formed in 1969.

Years later, as the African Nova Scotian community moved towards and into the twenty-first century, new agendas emerged in keeping with the growing maturity of the black population and a growing realization that, if much was achieved since the foundation years of notable ancestors, much was missing in an age when human rights were being propagated and promoted everywhere. In this context, many organizations and institutions emerged: the Black Educators Association, the Society for the Protection and Preservation of Black Culture in Nova Scotia (the Black Cultural Society), the Black Cultural Centre for Nova Scotia, the Black Business Consortium, the Black Professional Women's Group, the Congress of Black Women, the Association of Black Social Workers, the Afro-Canadian Caucus of Nova Scotia, the Black Learners Advisory Committee, the African Canadian Council of Education, and the Black Business Initiative.

In sum, the story of individuals and groups of African descent in what came to be known as Nova Scotia is the familiar one of a society grappling with the challenges of evolving times.

Chapter 1

The First Arrivals:
Slaves, Loyalists, Maroons, and Refugees

**RUNAWAY SLAVES WERE FREQUENTLY HUNTED DOWN,
CAPTURED, AND RETURNED TO FORMER OR NEW MASTERS**

The expansion of Europe overseas, from the fifteenth century onwards—
the period of exploitation by trading companies and missionary societies
promoting Christianity— brought considerable numbers of Africans to
the Americas. These Africans, pressed into service as captives of the West African
slave trade, were the forerunners of those who came later in larger numbers.
Using shipping and plantation records and other reliable sources, scholars have
concluded that between 1450 and 1850 the number of African slaves shipped to
North America, South America, and the Caribbean is somewhere between eleven
and fifteen million.

Any discussion of slavery must recognize that it was not limited to the enslavement of Africans by Europeans. Human beings were captured in wars and invasions in Western Asia and North Africa during the days of the Greek and Roman empires to provide labour for the ruling classes. Muslim invaders carried off African captives as slaves to Muslim lands like Arabia and Persia. Some of these captives eventually found their way to Europe through the expansion of trade. But in Europe there was little or no room for slave labour to advance economic prosperity from the fifteenth century onwards.

The expansion of Europe into the Americas opened up colossal opportunities for the exploitation of African and Aboriginal slave labour. It is in this context that in a four-hundred-year period millions of African slaves were pressed into brutal servitude in sugar, cotton, and tobacco plantations. As the black slave population grew—in many places surpassing the white population—slave revolts, slave runaways, slave acts of protest, and sabotage increased. The story of the slow but steady evolution from slavery to freedom—with the many ups and downs in between—is one that is told in the many studies of slavery in the Americas and the Caribbean, such as *From Slavery to Freedom* by John Hope Franklin.

For reasons pointed out in the Introduction, slavery in Nova Scotia was relatively short-lived, lasting from about 1686 to January 11, 1808, when a bill to legalize it failed to pass into law. There were no plantations in Nova Scotia to sustain it; slave labour in Nova Scotia and elsewhere in the Maritimes was not an economic necessity. Moreover, because of the absence of plantations, most slaves worked in domestic labour, or as skilled craftsmen and labourers in construction and shipbuilding. Thus, what the public saw in Nova Scotia was a picture of the "softer side" of slavery—if one can use such words to describe a brutalizing institution at a time when there was no such thing as equality between white and black. Nevertheless, the legacy of slavery affected race relations in Nova Scotia for centuries, as blacks suffered negative stereotyping and dehumanization in the eyes of whites.

As in the American colonies so too in the Maritime colonies, slaves did not always wait to be set free: they ran away to escape bondage and were often hunted down and brought before the courts. In some cases, the courts were sympathetic. In "The Slave in Canada," T. Watson Smith writes of a case brought before Chief Justice Blowers in Halifax in 1797 of a black woman slave from Annapolis: "At the trial the plaintiff proved a purchase of the Negro in New York as a slave," said the Chief Justice, "but as he could not prove that the seller had a legal right so to dispose of her, I directed the jury to find for the defendant, which they really did."

Ten years earlier, in 1787, a majority of the Nova Scotia legislature refused to legalize slavery. When the matter was raised again in 1808, as mentioned above, the legislature confirmed its position. Thus slavery was legally out in Nova Scotia. Its aftermath in race relations, however, is another matter altogether. As we turn to the three other early groups of blacks who came to Nova Scotia, the discussion of slavery remains relevant, for among them there were free persons as well as slaves and ex-slaves. They would have understood better in their day the reported statement of a slave in Halifax who, on being offered freedom by his master, said: "Master, you eated me when I was meat, and now you must pick me when I'm bone."

These three other groups of early black settlers—Black Loyalists, Maroons, and Black Refugees—all came as a result of factors and circumstances in their respective countries, the American colonies that became the United States and the British colony of Jamaica. The destination of Nova Scotia was chosen for them by the British government. They came not because of any declared loyalty to their oppressors but because of the offer of freedom. They came as unequals and quickly learned that the colonial government's offers and promises would not materialize into the freedom they had hoped for. During the long period of colonization and imperialism, unequals remained unequals for generations to come. The labels given to these groups are the legacy of governments, historians, and historical writings. With the passage of time, the boundaries between the groups became increasingly blurred, as the groups were subsumed in the shared African diasporic culture.

During the American War of Independence from Great Britain (1775–1783) the so-called Negro factor figured prominently in the calculations of the British. In the colony of Virginia, for example, 40 per cent of the population was made up of blacks. As the revolution progressed, three British proclamations invited blacks to defect to the British side. Ellen Gibson Wilson, in her book *The Loyal Blacks*, relates the words of Boston King, one of the prominent black personalities who came to Nova Scotia, when he crossed over to the British lines: "I began to feel the happiness of liberty, of which I knew nothing before."

David George, another prominent personality to come to Nova Scotia, also crossed over, taking the congregation of the Silver Bluff Baptist Church of South Carolina with him. Thomas Peters, a sergeant in the Black Pioneers, a separate black regiment created at the time, also crossed over to the British side. Peters features most prominently for his work in Nova Scotia and New Brunswick, in particular for the petition he drafted and submitted to the British government on behalf of fellow disaffected immigrants underlining broken promises.

Between 1775 and 1783 more than three thousand free blacks and former slaves came to Nova Scotia under British sponsorship for their deemed loyalty to the British cause in North America. At the end of the war in 1783 they came in large numbers, with documents identifying them as immigrants "to go to Nova Scotia or wherever else he [i.e., the British commander in chief] may think proper."

The spectacle of eighty-one vessels transporting black immigrants from New York to Nova Scotia in 1783 was an ironic flashback to the experiences of generations of these immigrants who had once been transported from Africa in slave ships under British oppression. Port Roseway (renamed Shelburne) was the principal destination in Nova Scotia. Its satellite town, Birchtown, was born out of the prevailing mentality that black immigrants should be kept in a segregated settlement. With a black population of about fifteen hundred, it soon grew into one of the largest concentrations of blacks outside Africa.

At the time of the first arrival of Loyalists, white and black, Nova Scotia was thinly populated, but it had abundant forests, agricultural lands, wildlife and fish. Shelburne stood on the North East Arm of a bay on the Atlantic; here the whites lived with their slaves and servants. Birchtown, located on the North West Arm, a mere three miles away, was designated for a segregated black population. Life began anew for all, with a frontier sense of starting from scratch: living on ships in the harbour, tents on land, shelters made of log, sod, and bark. Rations, implements, and settlement help were doled out on the basis of class and colour—the yardstick of the day and for years to come.

Shelburne prospered. By the end of 1783—only months after the arrival of the Loyalists—Governor Parr was lyrical with praise: eight hundred houses built, six hundred under construction, one hundred sailing vessels and wharfs built.

What of Birchtown? The census of 1784 spoke of a village of 1,522 inhabitants, with 38 occupations, no commerce, no storekeeper, 1 peddler, 209 labourers, 46 carpenters, 37 sawyers, 11 coopers, 15 sailors, and 20 people employed in shipbuilding as carpenters, caulkers, rope-makers, anchor-makers, and sailmakers. Between two and six were listed as blacksmiths, barbers, cooks, bakers, shoemakers, tailors, and chimney sweeps. And there was one each listed in the following categories: bricklayer, painter, mason, butcher, skinner, miller, tanner, gardener, seamstress, hatter, clothier, weaver, doctor, carman, gentleman's servant, coachman, and chair-maker. Thirty-one were listed as farmers.

Without capital, credit, or land, they had only their labour to sell. Many had to indenture themselves to white settlers for a fixed period in exchange for wages, food, and clothing.

As Ellen Gibson Wilson notes:

The free blacks were, in fact, a reservoir of cheap labour. Frequently unable to get work on the surrounding farms, they traveled considerable distances to find jobs. Most white settlers preferred casual labour to regular servants, and they did not always want to maintain the slaves they had brought. The small-scale farms, trades and industries did not make efficient use of large numbers of workers. Some of the slaves were sold to the United States or West Indies, and some were hired out. Others were simply turned out when the free provisions ran out.

Thus, for the 1,522 pioneering black settlers of Birchtown listed in 1784, there was no future in Birchtown. They had to move out into other areas of Nova Scotia and New Brunswick to survive—or move out of Nova Scotia altogether, which many of them did when 1,196 left for Sierra Leone in 1792. The Sierra Leone Company, incorporated in London in 1787, had received a charter for thirty-one years to establish a government and open up trade. The company's agent, John Clarkson, came to Nova Scotia and New Brunswick to recruit blacks who qualified to leave (that is, had no debts, were not indentured, and were free and willing to go).

Other segregated black communities soon appeared on the map of Nova Scotia: Brindley Town (near Digby, with significant numbers of former Black Pioneers, notably Thomas Peters and Murphy Still, both former sergeants), Little Tracadie (near Guysborough, under the leadership of Thomas Brownspriggs), and Preston (near Dartmouth).

The future of these communities for the next ten years, until the exodus to Sierra Leone in 1792, is intertwined with their heroic and heart-rending efforts to survive the rigours of racism, discrimination, and broken promises. Before coming to Nova Scotia, they had been promised free grants of land, implements and rations to tide them over, and employment opportunities. What they experienced were long delays in the processing of their grants, in many cases up to ten years. When the few received land grants, they were mostly ten acres for a family, in barren and distant areas. There were no title deeds for these grants, only licences denoting occupation. The white immigrants were granted from one hundred to one thousand acres of the best lands with full title. Blacks remained at the end of the queue with no faith in the promises or in the goodwill of government officials. The future as they saw it rested in both individual and community initiatives, in using their skills as craftsmen, in tilling their little allotments in isolated and distant places, in building churches and schools for upliftment of dignity, self worth, and enlightenment.

THE BLACK LOYALIST HERITAGE SOCIETY OPERATES A MUSEUM IN THE FORMER BIRCHTOWN

The story of the Black Loyalists does not, of course, end with the exodus to Sierra Leone in 1792. Their history in Sierra Leone is outside the scope of this book but is told in considerable detail by James W. St. G. Walker in *The Black Loyalists: The Search for a Promised Land in Nova Scotia and Sierra Leone, 1783–1870*. And it is worth remembering that a good number remained behind in Nova Scotia to put down roots and to contribute to the development of their adopted land. In recent years the Black Loyalist Heritage Society, spearheaded by Elizabeth Cromwell of Shelburne has done remarkable work on gathering information about the Black Loyalists and their descendants. This society was formed in 1991 to promote public recognition of Black Loyalists as one of the founding settler groups of Canada. Mention must also be made of the ground-breaking initiative of the Nova Scotia Archives and Records Management in producing the virtual exhibit entitled "African Nova Scotians in the Age of Slavery and Abolition" in 2004.

THE MAROON SETTLEMENT IN TRELAWNY TOWN, JAMAICA

On the Caribbean island of Jamaica, Africans first appeared in 1517 when Spaniards brought them as slaves. When the British conquered the island in 1655, some of these slaves took to the hills to maintain their independence as a proud and martial people. But there was only so much that they could do in an era that was not favourable towards them: the local people were conquered and subjected to British rule. Those, like the Maroons, who resisted conquest and subjugation waged a losing guerilla war against the colonial power, which had greater and more superior resources.

The result was that eventually the British dictated peace terms tantamount to surrender and shipped off the most recalcitrant of them, the Trelawny Maroons, to Nova Scotia on June 6, 1796, aboard three transport ships: *Dover*, *Mary*, and *Ann*. This group of 568 comprised 167 men who could bear arms, while 401 were old men, women, and children.

Governor John Wentworth had considerable interest in the Maroons for plans of his own, both personal and official. With the resumption of the Napoleonic wars in Europe, the defence of Halifax became a consideration and the fighting Maroon men an asset in the building of the Citadel Hill fortifications. Wentworth had property in the Preston area that became known as the Wentworth farm, later occupied by his progeny, the forerunner of the Colley family. He purchased 1,214 hectares of land in the Preston area to settle the Maroons in what he considered a military outpost. In another house named Maroon Hall, he provided residence for Colonel William Quarrell, Commissary General for the Maroons, and his deputy, Alexander Ochterlony. He also employed some Maroons in Government House in Halifax.

COLLEY FARM, ONCE GOVERNOR WENTWORTH'S PROPERTY

LEONARD PARKINSON, A MAROON CAPTAIN

But the majority of the Maroons resisted Wentworth's efforts to turn them into submissive, westernized, Christian farmers, labourers, and settlers: they refused offers to become indentured labourers; they refused to attend church or school. Theirs was a form of civil disobedience, an assertion of their heritage as free persons used to a lifestyle that did not include farming or manual labour. It was only under duress that they did work assigned to them, such as when the schoolmaster was instructed not to feed them. A few of them were willing to conform and were settled on a farm of one thousand acres in 1797. These few numbered about sixty by 1799. This Maroon settlement was in Boydville, in present Middle Sackville, and was also called Maroon Hill.

Wentworth's efforts to turn the majority of the Maroons into permanent settlers were opposed by both the Maroons and a number of landowners envious of
Wentworth's monopoly designs. Thus, 551 Maroons left for Sierra Leone aboard
the *Asia* on August 7, 1800.

It is difficult to say whether this number of 551 constituted all the Maroons
and their offspring in the Boydville settlement and the Preston area. Some
descendants later traced their lineage to the Maroon line as a result of co-min-
gling and co-existence. The authors have not at this stage gathered detailed
information on possible descendants and where they might be today, except for
the brief information on the Colley family gleaned through interviews in 1987-
88 with Charlotte Wilhemina Colley. Future researchers could well explore the
genealogical history of the Colley family tree beginning with the liaison between
Governor John Wentworth and his Maroon mistress, Sarah Colley; the birth
of their first offspring, James Wentworth Colley (1803-93); and the third generation beginning with James Wentworth Colley (1844-1905). According to
the information given by Charlotte Colley, her father, James Alexander Colley
(1874-1935), belonged to the fourth generation.

**MAROON HALL,
DARTMOUTH**

By the time the Maroons left for Sierra Leone, Nova Scotia had become a safe and geographically close haven for American blacks. Those who had immigrated as a result of the American Revolution left for Sierra Leone in 1792; so did the Trelawny Maroons of Jamaica in 1800. The vacuum created by the evacuated black settlements was quickly filled by some two thousand new black displaced persons who chose to claim refuge in a British colony. The War of 1812 between the United States of America and Great Britain was none of their making, but a proclamation by the commander of the British army in April 1814, inviting slaves and free blacks to emigrate with their families to either join the British forces or be sent as free settlers to British territories in North America or the West Indies, was hard to resist. As slaves and labourers they were aware of the pernicious situation in the United States, where slavery still existed and where there was no guarantee that the free could not be re-enslaved.

The result was that between 1813 and 1816 some two thousand American blacks, free and slave, arrived in the Maritimes to take up residence in New Brunswick and Nova Scotia. New Brunswick received between four and five hundred of this number. By the end of 1816 the number in Nova Scotia was 1,619. Their settlement areas at this time were principally Preston (924), Hammonds Plains (504), Halifax (115), and what is today called Beechville (76).

**NORTH PRESTON,
C.1930**

Their arrival and settlement were fraught with many difficulties, as well as considerable opposition from the white establishment. While the British government, operating through its military representatives in Bermuda, was adamant that these refugees of the War of 1812 should be received and settled in the Maritimes, the white establishment in Nova Scotia was reluctant and unwilling. Discrimination against blacks in land grants and employment opportunities had led to the exodus of previous black immigrants in 1792 and 1800, but a number almost equal to the refugees arriving in the years 1813-1816 had remained behind, bringing the total number of blacks to between four and five thousand. While the earlier immigrants were struggling to eke out a living in the segregated backwoods settlements of Preston, Hammonds Plains, and Beechville, tilling small areas for domestic and market gardening, undertaking seasonal part-time jobs, living virtually as tenants of the government under documents called licences of occupation, the newcomers horrified the majority whites as burdens on the state, competing for white jobs with their cheap subsistence labour. Watching them lining up for food, clothing and shelter at the poor house in Halifax or in quarantine on Melville Island, where the Armdale Yacht Club stands today, was enough to convince members of the Nova Scotia House of Assembly that these refugees were unfit to be in the colony:

> *the proportion of Africans already in this country is productive of many inconveniences; and that the introduction of more must tend to the discouragement of white labourers and servants, as well as to the establishment of a separate and marked class of people, unfitted by nature to this climate; or to an association with the rest of His Majesty's Colonists.*

Yet they stayed to prove this assessment wrong, overcame numerous obstacles, expanded their isolated settlements, merged in secular and spiritual initiatives, resisted the offers from time to time to follow the earlier groups to Sierra Leone. Only in 1821 did ninety-five of this number agree to emigrate to Trinidad. The rest stayed and over the centuries left their indelible marks on the history of Nova Scotia. The literature on their remarkable journey and their considerable success is already impressive and growing. Their place in Nova Scotia society, not yet completely bereft of the occasional flashback to their colonial experience, is nonetheless confirmed and they are acknowledged as a founding people and as contributing citizens. In the assessment of Burnley A. Jones, an articulate and vocal member of the black community, instead of freedom and independence, which drew free blacks to Nova Scotia, they experienced servitude and discrimination. While their labour helped to build roads and buildings and the fortunes of white society, they remained on the periphery of Nova Scotian society.

The remaining pages of this book will, of necessity, be a selective presentation of the intertwining histories of these black communities, which faced great adversity but which nevertheless made great contributions to the history of Nova Scotia.

Chapter 2

Baptism by Fire:
David George, Richard Preston, and Other Pioneers in Church Work

OUTDOOR BAPTISM, EAST PRESTON, 1976

I n the history of African Nova Scotians, no other institution has had the pervading influence of the black Baptist church. This chapter will deal with the contribution of two notable personalities and an organization that has withstood the test of time for 150 years. The personalities are David George (1743–1810) and Richard Preston (1790–1861); the organization is the African United Baptist Association (AUBA) which was founded on September 1, 1854.

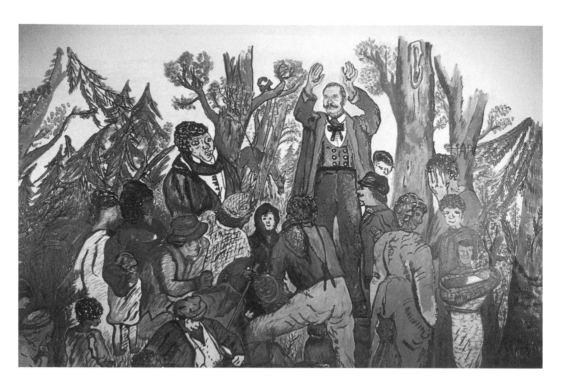

**DAVID GEORGE,
THE FIRST BLACK
BAPTIST PREACHER
IN NOVA SCOTIA**

David George was born in Essex County, Virginia, the son of slave parents from Africa. As a young man in the 1770s he spent some years at a trading post in Silver Bluff, South Carolina, where he came under the influence of the Silver Bluff Baptist Church and served as an elder, a pastor, and a leading member of the congregation. Through contacts and friendly officials during the American War of Independence, including the British commander in Charleston, South Carolina, David George obtained the necessary documents certifying that he was a British subject. He and his family, a few other blacks, and some five hundred white persons were in the first batch of Loyalist emigrants to sail from Charleston in October 1782, arriving in Halifax the following month. Through the assistance of an organization formed in New York by Loyalist families, called the Port Roseway Associates, David George left for Port Roseway (later Shelburne) in June 1783.

By the time David George reached Shelburne town, lots were being laid out by land surveyor Benjamin Marston, and a large convoy of ships had arrived from New York. In days the population of the town rose from a few hundred to over four thousand. Settling this large influx of people on land grants proved very difficult. Friction and unruliness were the order of the day. It was in this frontier atmosphere that David George took up his mantle as a Baptist preacher and held outdoor meetings for both white and black, as he had done at Silver Bluff. However, this time the result was different: he was ordered by the white settlers to leave the town and preach in the woods.

A month after his arrival in Shelburne, David George was given a small grant of land, about one-quarter of an acre, by Nova Scotia governor John Parr, when the governor visited this pioneer settlement. Evidently, George must have made an impression on the governor when he and his family were put up in Halifax. The family had remained behind when George went on to Shelburne. Now, with the governor's help, they were united. The plot of land for the family was located to the north of Shelburne, a few miles from the town.

In this atmosphere of social and economic friction between white and black settlers, Governor Parr instructed the land surveyor to establish a separate settlement for the black settlers, some three to four miles from the centre of Shelburne. This led to the founding of Birchtown, as discussed in Chapter 1. Here the black settlers, under new leaders, were organized in companies to work in Shelburne, building roads and government buildings, clearing the land, and eking out a living in whatever jobs were available at low wages. Their contribution to the development of the town would come to work against them in less than a year.

Over this time, David George carried out his pastoral work in a modest meeting house in Shelburne, baptizing both whites and blacks, with the help of his wife and a few supporters. It was in such unassuming circumstances that David George's work made him the founder of the first black Baptist church in all of Canada. The price he paid was quite severe. In July 1784, his home and property, including the small church, were attacked and destroyed by thousands of white settlers. On July 26, 1784, this mob of disbanded soldiers rose against all the free blacks in Shelburne, blaming them for taking jobs and providing cheap labour. The rioting soon spread to Birchtown and nearby towns. When it subsided towards the end of the year, George and his family returned to what remained of their dwelling in Shelburne to resume the work of his ministry. His reputation had spread to the point where nearby and more distant towns invited him to preach; the New Light churches allowed him the use of their premises, and the newly established province of New Brunswick allowed him to pioneer his Baptist work in its capital, Fredericton, under special licence. George's itinerant ministry took him to other parts of New Brunswick and to many parts of Nova Scotia, notably Halifax, the Annapolis Valley, and the Preston area.

David George's life and work in Nova Scotia and New Brunswick must be seen in the context of the struggle of Black Loyalists in general as outlined in Chapter 1, and particularly in relation to the decade-long stay of those who left for Sierra Leone in 1792 in search of better opportunities. His courageous example of standing up for the Baptist church and his itinerant tours had a lasting influence on the work of the AUBA in later years. He can also be seen as a role model through his rise from slavery to church and community leadership, his itinerant pastorate in Nova Scotia and New Brunswick, his unflagging faith in the work he was doing in spite of attacks on his person, his family, his church, and his congregation. Taken together, his short stay (1782–1792) and his durable legacy represent for both black and white adherents a lasting lesson in how not to give up.

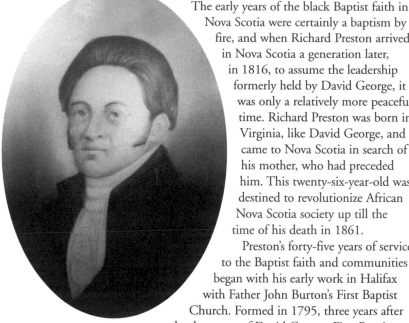

RICHARD PRESTON, PIONEERING PREACHER AND FOUNDER OF THE AFRICAN UNITED BAPTIST ASSOCIATION

The early years of the black Baptist faith in Nova Scotia were certainly a baptism by fire, and when Richard Preston arrived in Nova Scotia a generation later, in 1816, to assume the leadership formerly held by David George, it was only a relatively more peaceful time. Richard Preston was born in Virginia, like David George, and came to Nova Scotia in search of his mother, who had preceded him. This twenty-six-year-old was destined to revolutionize African Nova Scotia society up till the time of his death in 1861.

Preston's forty-five years of service to the Baptist faith and communities began with his early work in Halifax with Father John Burton's First Baptist Church. Formed in 1795, three years after the departure of David George, First Baptist was the oldest black Baptist congregation in Halifax. There was a second congregation in Hammonds Plains, some twenty kilometres from Halifax, where a sizeable black community lived. It was here that Richard Preston concentrated his efforts, with remarkable success.

At the time, Father Burton was much criticized by white Baptists for working with black church members and for licensing unqualified black church members as elders and preachers. This criticism extended to Richard Preston, who was deemed by his critics to lack the necessary qualifications for the work he was doing. In spite of this criticism Richard Preston served for three years (1821–24) as the first black delegate to the Maritime Baptist Association. However, when an increasing number of new white members joined Burton's church it became clear that black members were no longer welcome, and black Baptists began planning to organize their own church. They looked to Richard Preston, who had been issued a licence to preach by Burton in 1823. These black Baptists— William Henry, Jacob Allen, John Hamilton, Prince William Sport, and Joseph Campbell—decided to raise funds to build an independent black Baptist church in Halifax and send Preston to England to study for ordination.

Preston landed in Liverpool on April 15, 1831, on his way to London, where he was ordained in the Grafton Church chapel on May 8, 1832, by the West London Baptist Association. He raised £650 in London to build the Cornwallis Street African Baptist Church in Halifax later that year. The committee of black Baptists realized its objective with the appointment of Rev. Richard Preston as the first pastor.

FORMATION OF THE AFRICAN UNITED BAPTIST ASSOCIATION

In addition to helping found eleven black Baptist churches in Nova Scotia in twenty years, Richard Preston's monumental achievement was the formation in 1854 of the African United Baptist Association, an umbrella organization based primarily on the notion that province-wide affiliation and spiritual leadership were needed to unite the majority of the black population. The unity of the total black population was never affected by the fact that a minority joined other denominations; in secular activities and organizations, cooperation was markedly free of religious divisions.

The Anglican and Methodist denominations, with considerable funds at their disposal, were not absent from the scene. Through its Society for the Propagation of the Gospel (established in Nova Scotia in 1749), the Anglican church supported black settlers with food and clothing. It handpicked blacks to provide religious instruction to other blacks in their homes. One such instructor was Joseph Leonard. The Methodists did the same. They appointed Moses Wilkinson, a blind preacher, to build a church in Birchtown at the same time as David George built his. These efforts were designed for segregated congregations under white leadership, but the majority of Blacks veered towards Baptist initiatives. They were led by their own and they emphasized black identity, black freedom, and black independence—three attributes that mattered throughout the black experience.

The AUBA was founded in the picturesque setting of Granville Mountain, not far from Inglewood (Bridgetown), with thirty-six delegates present. There were three ordained ministers present—Rev. Richard Preston (Halifax), Rev. John Hamilton (Hammonds Plains), and Rev. Henry Jackson (Bear River) along with licensed ministers, deacons, and elders. Richard Preston's designation in the minutes of the inaugural meeting was "Bishop."

The association's first annual convention was held on its first anniversary, in 1855, with the Rev. Henry Jackson elected as the organization's first moderator and Septimus Clarke as first clerk. The title conferred upon the Cornwallis Street Baptist Church was "Mother Church" of the association, a title that lives on as a tribute to its visionary founder.

Since 1855 the highlight in the life and work of the AUBA and its member churches has been the annual convention held in different venues in a celebratory atmosphere replete with dignity, decorum, and celebration. In the last 150 years there have been only a few years when administrative difficulties led to the postponement of this event. The AUBA has been, and continues to be, the most outstanding beacon of the Nova Scotia black experience since the mid-nineteenth century. It has had its ups and downs, but it has endured. What is remarkable is that over a period of 150 years the AUBA has produced outstanding leaders in its pastors, moderators, and members.

The member churches of the AUBA are more than places of worship. They are institutions that members as well as non-members can turn to for help, guidance, and comfort. Historically, the building of new churches in existing and expanding settlements was a sign that black communities were mobilizing their resources to use existing opportunities as well as to initiate new ones. Church and community histories have gone hand in hand for African Nova Scotians, largely because the churches of the AUBA were led by blacks and symbolized black identity, freedom, and independence.

PIONEERS IN CHURCH WORK

The African Methodist church built in 1784–85 by Moses Wilkinson in Birchtown and the Baptist church built by David George in Shelburne in 1785 were short-lived, as both these pastors left for Sierra Leone in 1792. The oldest remaining black churches in Nova Scotia were the Windsor Plains Baptist Church, organized in 1812, and the Tracadie Church, organized in 1822. Though seemingly unimposing from the outside and located on a small lot on Cornwallis Street, the "Mother Church" features prominently in the annals of the black experience in Nova Scotia. Organized on April 14, 1832, and rebuilt in 1914, the African Baptist Church was renamed by statute in 1892 as the Cornwallis Street Baptist Church. It was from this base that Richard Preston not only organized some twelve churches but ran the Anglo-African Mutual Improvement Aid Association (1842), the Negro Abolition Society (1846), and the African United Baptist Association (1854). (Many notable personalities connected with the work of this church, such as James R. Johnston, J. A. R. Kinney, William A. White, and William Pearly Oliver, appear in later sections of this book).

CORNWALLIS STREET UNITED BAPTIST CHURCH DURING A THANKSGIVING SERVICE, c.1950

The Emmanuel Baptist Church was founded in 1845 in Upper Hammonds Plains, in an area settled by the Black Refugees who arrived from the United States as a result of the War of 1812. As in other black settlements in Nova Scotia, the Baptist church was the embodiment of the community. Although located some twenty kilometers from Halifax, the Emmanuel Baptist Church and its community were closely tied to the events, institutions, and personalities of the capital city. Rev. William Parker Clayton's account of the church, *Whatever Your Will, Lord*, tells us of the well-known superintendent of the Cornwallis Street Baptist Church, Deacon Clarence H. Johnston, who extended his services and enthusiasm to the church and people of Upper Hammonds Plains.

**EAST PRESTON
UNITED BAPTIST
CHURCH, ONE OF
ELEVEN CHURCHES
FOUNDED BY
RICHARD PRESTON**

Carolyn G. Thomas, a notable black church historian and second woman moderator of the AUBA, has edited a book, under the title *Reflections*, to mark the 150th anniversary of the East Preston United Baptist Church. From this book we learn that this church was founded in 1842 by Richard Preston and that its original name was First Preston Church. The list of pastors who have served this church from 1842 to 1995 includes Richard Preston, James Thomas, George Neale, Edward Dixon, John Smith, Arthur Wyse, Donald D. Skeir, and Glenn Gray. Equally impressive is the list of deacons whose contribution to the community transcended the church to include secular organizations, service clubs, and social and economic development.

Another church founded by Richard Preston was the Digby Joggins Church, which was founded in 1853. It served an area that was once a thriving settlement during the Loyalist immigration to Brindley Town, close to Digby. Among other associations, the area was once occupied by some of the black pioneers led by Sergeant Thomas Peters.

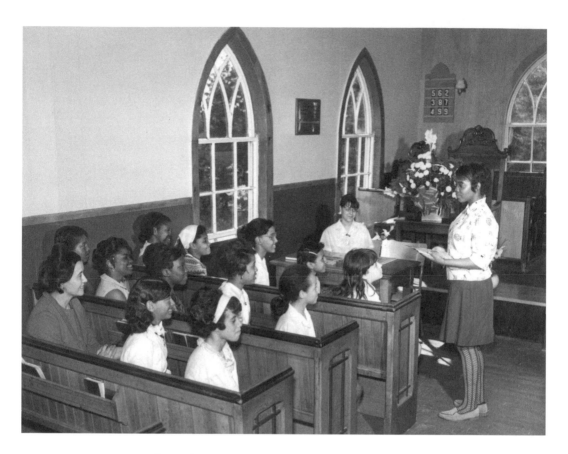

BEECHVILLE UNITED BAPTIST CHURCH

Pearleen Oliver's book, *Song of the Spirit: An Historical Narrative on the History of the Beechville United Baptist Church, 150th Anniversary, 1844-1994* is another valuable compilation from the pen of a distinguished Baptist church historian. As in the accounts given above, the list of ordained ministers and church deacons who served Beechville over the period of 150 years is an affirmation of leadership and strength. While all served with distinction in Beechville, an area that began as a black community primarily in the refugee period after 1812, some became associated actively with other churches over the years. In addition to Richard Preston, such other names as Rev. William A. White, Rev. William P. Oliver, Rev. Wellington N. States, and Rev. Willard P. Clayton feature prominently among the later Baptist pastors. Among the numerous personalities from Beechville who have made their mark in the Nova Scotia black experience must be included such names as William Golar, who left Beechville to study in the United States, became Professor of Ancient Languages in Livingstone College, Salsbury, North Carolina, and ended as president of that institution; Marie Hamilton; and Pearleen Oliver.

Marie Hamilton (1912–93) taught school at North Preston, Cherry Brook, Hammonds Plains, and Beechville. Between 1957 and 1990 she served as clerk of the Beechville church, worked with the Ladies Auxiliary of the church, and was the force behind the North End Halifax Library Women's Group. A quiet and unassuming person, Marie Hamilton spent her later years in her house on

Russell Street in Halifax, continuing to counsel and to serve social causes, for all of which she was both respected and rewarded. Among her many awards were the Queen's Jubilee Medal (1977), the Person's Award (1983), and the honorary degree of Doctor of Humane Letters from Mount Saint Vincent University (1985).

PEARLEEN OLIVER AT BEECHVILLE BAPTIST CHURCH

Althea Pearleen Oliver was born in Cook's Cove, Guysborough, Nova Scotia, in 1918, the daughter of Joseph Borden and Clara Belle. In 1936 she was the first black student to graduate from the New Glasgow High School. In the same year she married the Rev. William Pearly Oliver. Pearleen Oliver wanted to become a nurse after graduation but was denied the opportunity because of her race. She did something about that in later years, directing her energies to remove the barriers against black girls entering the nursing profession. She took her campaign on the road, speaking to business and service clubs, church groups, community organizations, and anyone who would listen. Her reward came when Ruth Bailey of Toronto and Gwen Barton of Halifax graduated from the Children's Hospital in Halifax in September 1948. Pearleen Oliver also protested against the stereotyping of blacks in the story of "Black Sambo" used in class readers, and was in the vanguard of protest when Viola Desmond was arrested and imprisoned on November 8, 1946, for sitting downstairs in New Glasgow's Roseland Theatre, instead of in the balcony reserved for black customers.

The first woman to have held the position of supervisor of the Baptist Young Peoples' Union (1945-48), and the first woman to be elected Moderator of the AUBA, Pearleen Oliver holds the distinction of being the most prolific author of the black Baptist experience in Nova Scotia.

Nestled in a quiet corner of Nova Scotia is the town of New Glasgow in Pictou County, first home of Scottish immigrants who arrived aboard the *Hector* in 1773, and whose arrival was predated by pioneering blacks of the pre-Loyalist era. In the impressive news sheet entitled "Native Born: A Brief History of the Black Presence in Pictou County," a black community reunion publication of 1990, reference is made to the formation of the first black church, the Second Baptist Church, in 1903. The charter members were seven in number: John J. Williams, Henrietta Jordan, J. W. Borden, Susanne Reddick, Fred Sheppard and M. J. Borden. Assisted by Rev. William A. White, they purchased a piece of land on Washington Street and built a small church. Over the years the small church survived. During the thirteen-year pastorate of the Rev. Wellington N. States, the small church was replaced by a larger structure which opened in 1913.

What is remarkable in this pastoral setting, which has experienced its fair share of racial friction and bigotry over centuries, is that the influence of church and community has produced personalities and achievements that have transcended rural Nova Scotia into other parts of the country and beyond. Peter J. Paris is a case in point. Born in New Glasgow in 1933, he went on to obtain the BA and Bachelor of Divinity degrees from Acadia University and the MA and PhD degrees from the University of Chicago. He was ordained in 1959 by the AUBA. Since 1985 he has held the position of Elmer G. Homrighausen Professor of Christian Social Ethics in the Princeton Theological Seminary. Before that he was attached to the Vanderbilt Divinity School and Howard University School of Religion, all in the USA.

Other famous names, which appear in other parts of this volume, associated with the Pictou County church and community are Carrie Best, founder of the *Clarion* newspaper; her son Calbert Best, one time Canadian high commissioner in Trinidad and Tobago; George Borden, captain in the Canadian Armed Forces; his brother Walter Borden, internationally renowned Canadian actor and playwright; Delmore "Buddy" Daye, Canadian Junior Lightweight Boxing Champion; and Francis Dorrington, New Glasgow town councillor and deputy mayor for many years.

In a research article entitled "A Tale of Three Churches: Ethnic Architecture in Sydney, Nova Scotia," Elizabeth Beaton writes about St. Phillip's African Orthodox Church in Whitney Pier, organized in 1921 and located on Hankard Road. Beaton describes it as the only African Orthodox parish in Canada, and places it in its social context in the following words:

St. Philip's Church is the focal point for the Black community in Sydney, which now numbers about 250 families. The community, which developed as a result of Sydney's industrialization, is varied in its origins. The first Blacks to work in the steel plant came from Alabama in 1899, but most left Cape Breton soon after their arrival.... The largest immigration of Blacks was composed of West Indians.... Most were able to find jobs in Cape Breton's industrial area. In Sydney, the West Indian culture became the dominant pattern.... The West Indians married with the other Blacks and formed a community in the area adjacent to the steel plant known as the "Coke Ovens," where they are presently the most obviously segregated ethnic group in Whitney Pier.

ARCHPRIEST GEORGE FRANCIS, LONGTIME PRIEST OF ST. PHILIP'S AFRICAN ORTHODOX CHURCH

While many personalities have been associated with the work of St. Philip's Church, one of the most remarkable was Venerable Archpriest George A. Francis, who served it and the community for forty-two years from September 1, 1940, until his death on June 13, 1982. Francis was born in Santiago, Cuba, on February 16, 1908, and came to Cape Breton after completing high school and theological studies in New York City. He was elevated to the position of canon in 1949 and vicar general in 1970. Among his vast community services were the Children's Aid Society, the Canadian Red Cross, and the Canadian Cancer Society. His daughter, Mayann Francis is presently chief executive officer of the Nova Scotia Human Rights Commission.

ARCHBISHOP VINCENT M. WATERMAN INSIDE ST. PHILIP'S AFRICAN ORTHODOX CHURCH

Archbishop Vincent M. Waterman succeeded Archpriest George Francis in 1983. Born in Barbados and educated in New York, he was ordained in the priesthood in 1964 and elevated to the office of archbishop in New York City in 1994. His volunteer services since 1983 are quite extensive and include membership on the boards of the Red Cross Society, the Cancer Society, the United Way, the Sydney Boys and Girls Club, the Multicultural Association of Nova Scotia, the John Howard Society, and the Advisory Board of Drug Dependency Services. He is married to the former Isabel Francis, daughter of Archpriest George Francis.

Later Pastors

THE EXECUTIVE COMMITTEE OF THE AFRICAN UNITED BAPTIST ASSOCIATION, 1920
BACK ROW (L-R): J. A. R. KINNEY, WELLINGON STATES
FRONT ROW (L-R): DEACON JOHNSON, REV. A. A. WYSE, REV. W. A. WHITE

In a photograph of the executive committee of the AUBA taken in 1919–20, the church personalities and pastors shown are James A. R. Kinney (secretary), Rev. W. N. States (assistant secretary), Thomas P. Johnson (treasurer), Rev. A. A. Wyse (moderator), and Rev. W. A. White (vice-moderator). Taken individually and collectively, these men represented the dynamism of the Baptist faith in Nova Scotia, in the period when the world was just beginning to recover from the ravages of World War I. Each one of them has left a tremendous legacy that is remembered and revered to this day.

In this group two were lay persons: Deacon Thomas P. Johnson, who served the AUBA as treasurer from 1915 to 1936, and J. A. R. Kinney. Both served on the first board set up in 1914 to build the Halifax Industrial School and Home to accommodate children in need of shelter, and both were foundation trustees of the Nova Scotia Home for Coloured Children, which opened in Westphal in 1921. J. A. R. Kinney, who is profiled in Chapter 6, was the first black Nova Scotian to graduate from the Maritime Business School. Notably, in the history of the AUBA, Kinney served as clerk from 1916–21 and later as treasurer (1939-40). Both Johnson and Kinney were ardent proponents of education for advancement, and they put their energies and strategies to good purpose to help the youth and the homeless.

Of the three pastors in the group, Rev. Wellington Naey States (1877-1927) was the first to serve as field missionary for the AUBA. Born in Wolfville, Nova Scotia, on November 1, 1877, he lost his mother when he was three and his father when he was nine. Life with his white maternal grandparents was hard, and young Wellington took to the seas at age fourteen, after a few years at school where he excelled in carpentry. Helped later by his paternal grandparents in Mount Denson, he enrolled at Horton Academy in Wolfville to study theology. He obtained a licence to preach from the Cornwallis Street Baptist Church in 1898 and later proceeded to serve Baptist churches in the Bridgetown area. He was ordained by the Rev. G. Coulter White at Inglewood Church in 1899, four years before the ordination of William Andrew White. For twenty-eight years he served the Baptist churches of Nova Scotia, for at least nine of them taking his portable organ and his carpentry tools from church to church. He died on May 3, 1927. On that occasion the Halifax *Chronicle-Herald* ran the following tribute:

He was a most practical man of varied activities with high executive ability—by trade he was a carpenter, and there is hardly a colored church in Nova Scotia that has not felt his hand as a builder. He built churches in New Glasgow, Hammonds Plains, Granville Ferry and Delaps Cove, besides repairing and remodeling the ones in Acaciaville, Tracadie, Sunnyville, Kentville, Beechville, Africville, Cherrybrook and Dartmouth—a man who made such gigantic sacrifices in physical strength that at the early age of fifty years the sun of his life has set.

The legacy of States and his family—wife Muriel, son Coulter, and daughters Leota and Patricia—lived on for decades in their contributions to church, labour, education, and society. His granddaughter, Sherrolynn Riley, retired from school teaching, studied theology, and was ordained Baptist pastor in November 2003. Thus, the work begun by Rev. Wellington States lives on even today.

In a similar vein, there are parallels here with the life, work, and legacy of Rev. William Andrew White (1874-1936). Born in Virginia, William White enrolled at Acadia University, Wolfville, in 1899 and was ordained in 1903. His first pastorate was served in New Glasgow until he was assigned to the Zion Baptist Church in Truro in 1905. His twelve-year service there was interrupted by a call to service overseas as chaplain to the No. 2 Construction Battalion in 1917. Rev. White's formidable contribution to church history includes eight years as clerk of the AUBA and two years as moderator (1929-31).

When he assumed the mantle of moderator at the beginning of the Great Depression, the minutes of the AUBA record the enthusiasm of a pastor who had been through tough times here and abroad but still sounded the clarion call of faith, hope, and justice:

> It is our hope that we are at the beginning of a new era of prosperity in the churches, and among our people as a whole. If this is to become reality, there are some things which must be borne in mind by all members and adherents of the Association. First, we would stress on the necessity for the united efforts on the part of all those who would see the work progress. The selection of a group of officers, however capable they may be, is not sufficient to accomplish the task before us. Every individual must hold himself in readiness to do his bit for the advancement of all. There must be faith in the task we have assigned ourselves.

WILLIAM A. WHITE JR.

White's years as pastor of the Mother Church, Cornwallis Street Baptist Church (1919-36), brought him to the pinnacle of the black Baptist church in Nova Scotia. Here he found fulfillment for his uncompromising Christian faith, his melodious voice, and his message to the masses. The message was heeded deservedly: on May 28, 1936, Acadia University awarded him with an honorary doctorate. When he died on September 9, 1936, the province responded with a fond and massive farewell.

Here, too, the legacy lived on in the later work of his wife, Izie (later Mrs. C. H. Johnston), and his children. His famous daughter, Portia White (1911-68), and his son, Lorne White (b. 1928), have earned prominent places on the provincial and national scenes. And Portia White, who will be discussed in a later chapter, was acclaimed internationally. His other daughter Helena White (later Mrs. Clifford Oliver), was the mother of Nova Scotia's first black senator, Donald Oliver. William Andrew White (son), prominent personnel manager in Ontario, received the Order of Canada. Mildred Porter (daughter) spent most of her adult life in Ohio, where she was a prominent chemist, noted for her professional work in preventing gun barrels from rusting. Nettie Clarke (daughter) was a supervisor in the federal service, and George Albert White (son) was a long-serving certified drug clerk in Halifax. This list of accomplishments, incomplete and necessarily brief, is a testament to the power of positive family environment.

Of the executive committee of 1919-20 with which this section began, the name of Rev. A. A. Wyse (1867-1953) remains. He had an extremely long and successful pastorate at the East Preston United Baptist Church, which lasted for forty-three years beginning in 1911 with a short period of licentiate till 1915. His ordination in 1915 was, however, met with some opposition in the AUBA, whose council was convened on February 15, 1915, to deliberate on the matter. No reasons were given for the hold-up of the ordination of the forty-eight-year-old licentiate, and he went on to serve well into his eighties. After his death, he was succeeded by Rev. Donald D. Skeir (1953-95).

Among the later pastoral pioneers, four deserve special mention: William Oliver, Donald Skeir, Donald Fairfax, and Willard Clayton.

**WILLIAM AND
PEARLEEN OLIVER
AT HOME IN
LUCASVILLE, 1978**

In fifty-three years of pastoral services in Nova Scotia, William Pearly Oliver ranks foremost in almost every field of church and related service open to a Baptist pastor. He bestrode the field with dignity and diplomatic forthrightness, which made him one of the best known personalities in Nova Scotia. He was born in Wolfville, Nova Scotia, on February 11, 1912. His father, Clifford Oliver, worked in the farm of Acadia University. William Oliver graduated with a Bachelor of Divinity degree in 1936, and was ordained in the same year. After a short stint in Windsor Plains, he was called to the Cornwallis Street church in 1936. Until his death in 1989, he served the Baptist church in every position open to a pastor, including supervisor of the Baptist Young People's Union, moderator of the AUBA, and chairman of the Urban and Rural Life Committee of the AUBA. His contribution went beyond the church to include public service. Rev. Oliver's name is associated with the formation of the Nova Scotia Association for the Advancement of Coloured People (1945), the Black United Front (1969), the Black Cultural Society of Nova Scotia (1977), and the Black Cultural Centre of Nova Scotia (1983). On July 26, 1986, Rev. Oliver and his wife, Pearleen Oliver, celebrated a remarkable triple golden anniversary at Acadia University: fifty years of marriage, fifty years of Christian ministry, and fifty years of sustained and selfless service to community. The W. P. Oliver Wall of Honour was set up at the centre after his death to commemorate his life and work, and to recognize the contributions made by individuals to enhance the aspirations of the black community.

DONALD SKEIR WITH DOUG SKINNER AND JOHNNY SAUNDERS, 1960

Donald D. Skeir was born in Halifax on November 23, 1926. He was educated in the city school system and later studied theology at Acadia University and special education at Dalhousie University. He was ordained at East Preston in 1951. His record of church service was long and impressive: pastor for the Preston and Cherrybrook churches for over forty-two years, clerk of the AUBA, moderator of the AUBA for three terms, and treasurer of the AUBA for nine years. He also found the time and energy to teach in the Bedford school system for twenty-seven years (1961-88). His service on boards promoting related social justice issues included work with the Nova Scotia Home for Coloured Children, the Black United Front, and the Black Cultural Society for Nova Scotia. An avid historian and superb orator, the Rev. Dr. Donald D. Skeir died on October 10, 1999.

DONALD AND MARJORIE FAIRFAX

Donald E. Fairfax was born in Cherrybrook, Halifax County. While working in Halifax his musical interest and talents drew him to the Cornwallis Street Baptist Church, where Portia White was the organist and Rev. W. P. Oliver the pastor. One step led to the other and by 1941 he found himself in Horton Academy of Acadia University studying theology. Two years later he was in the Voice Department of the Conservatory of Music in Halifax pursuing the other interest in his life. Shortly afterwards he accepted a call for three years to work as pastor of Shiloh Baptist Church in Edmonton. On his return, he took up the position of pastor of the Victoria Road United Baptist Church in 1947, serving this church with utter dedication for forty-four years as of February 1991. He also served the Lucasville United Baptist Church for over twenty-five years. Now retired, Dr. Fairfax continues to reside in Dartmouth.

During these years he served in many positions in church and societal service: four terms as moderator of the AUBA, principal of the Nelson Wynder School in North Preston, chairman of the Board of Directors of the Nova Scotia Home for Coloured Children for nine years, board member of the Nova Scotia Mental Health Association, and commissioner of the Nova Scotia Human Rights Commission.

In the midst of all this, and much more, Rev. Fairfax had a day job at the Nova Scotia Hospital from 1960 to 1985, showing clearly that church and public service required supplementary income to support a family of six children. Wives of pastors have served with distinction and Marjorie (Tynes) Fairfax was no exception. An accomplished musician herself and a graduate of the Halifax Conservatory of Music, Mrs. Fairfax served as Church Organist of the Victoria Road Baptist Church, taught Sunday school, was active in the Ladies Auxiliary of the AUBA, and was a charter member of the Women's Missionary Society. The Marjorie J. Fairfax Music Scholarship at Victoria Road Church is a testament to her accomplishments and inspiration. The Fairfaxes have received many honours. Rev. Fairfax was named to the Order of Canada in 1990.

DR. WILLARD P. CLAYTON

Dr. Willard P. Clayton was born in 1921. He was ordained in the Emmanuel Baptist Church in Hammonds Plains in 1952. While serving over the years in many pastorates in Nova Scotia and New Brunswick, Willard Clayton studied continually, obtaining degrees in arts, divinity, education, and a doctorate in religion from Geneva Theological College in South Carolina. These accomplishments were not handed to him on a silver platter. With a grade 4 education he worked in the woods of Hammonds Plains with his father. In his last teen years he attended night school in Halifax, then joined the army and served abroad during World War II. On being demobilized in 1945 he entered Horton Academy, then Acadia University, and the degrees mentioned above followed in succession. Along with all this, he too, like Revs. Skeir and Fairfax took to school teaching, serving for twenty-three years, some as vice-principal.

JEAN CLAYTON

As for the church, Rev. Clayton was pastor of Emmanuel Baptist Church from 1950 to 1958 and from 1982 onwards. On the death of Rev. Oliver in 1989, Rev. Clayton took over the pastorate of Beechville. His wife, Jean Clayton, has been, in addition to her role in church, a most active practitioner of social justice work, having served as a human rights officer of the Nova Scotia Human Rights Commission and as an investigative officer of the Federal Human Rights Commission, as well as a project officer for the United Way. The Claytons, now in retirement, continue to reside in Dartmouth.

Chapter 4

Publishing Pioneers:
The Advocate, the Gleaner, and the Clarion

THE KEITH BUILDING, HOME OF *THE ATLANTIC ADVOCATE*

The Nova Scotia black communities have long made good use of networking, publicity, and advocacy to promote their activities. In this regard, early publishing activities played an important part. Nova Scotia's first periodical devoted to the interests of the black population was *The Atlantic Advocate*. In 1992 Philip Hartling of the Public Archives of Nova Scotia prepared an exhibition on the *Advocate*, which included excellent biographical notes on the individuals associated with the paper. These notes are an invaluable resource for the history of African Nova Scotian publishing.

One name that stands out in the biographical notes is that of Mowbray Fitzgerald Jemmott. The Jemmott family name is often associated with school teaching in Africville. But here we learn much more: that he was born in Bridgetown, Barbados, and that he taught school there and later for two years in Newfoundland before coming to Nova Scotia. Most importantly, we learn that M. F. Jemmott was the first editor of *The Atlantic Advocate*, and that the first location of this publication was his residence at 58 Gottingen Street. The business later moved to Wilfred and Miriam DeCosta's house, then to the Keith building (now the Green Lantern Building) on Barrington Street, and finally to Dr. Clement Courtenay Ligoure's house at 166 North Street. The first issue appeared in April 1915 and the last around May-June 1917. Over time, it varied in length from eight pages to sixteen. Single issues were sold for 10¢ and annual subscriptions for $1.00 in Canada or $1.20 elsewhere. The paper's demise in 1917 was presumably the result of the high cost of printing and materials during wartime, as well as the absence of some of the staff, who were overseas contributing to the war effort.

Many personalities associated with *The Atlantic Advocate* appear in other areas of black history: Dr. Clement Ligoure is associated with the medical profession; George Roache with business; Wilfred A. DeCosta, Ethelbert Lionel Cross, and William Thomas with the No. 2 Construction Battalion in World War I. In Calvin Ruck's *The Black Battalion, 1916-1920: Canada's Best Kept Military Secret*, Wilfred DeCosta is listed as a sergeant-major, and William Thomas as a sergeant. E. L. Cross is not listed, but according to Philip Hartling, he was a sergeant born in the British West Indies; his next-of-kin was Mrs. Eloise Cross, San Fernando, Trinidad. By June 1916, he was living in Halifax.

According to Hartling, it was Wilfred DeCosta who first proposed the launching of a black periodical in Halifax. In Hartling's words, the *Advocate* "covered a wide range of topics—historical, religious, economic, political, military, literary (fiction, poetry, songs), social and local. Community notes were received from across Nova Scotia, including Amherst, Digby, Halifax, Hammonds Plains, Liverpool, Shelburne, Westville, Weymouth and Wolfville; Saint John, New Brunswick; Montreal, Quebec; and Chatham and Windsor, Ontario."

The paper's editorial purpose was clearly stated in the first issue, published in April 1915:

> We earnestly hope that all our friends will give the Atlantic Advocate the favorable consideration which it deserves; and the publishers in their turn shall do their utmost to place in the columns of their periodical just such news as they desire....
>
> The Atlantic Advocate aims to show our people the need of unity, the desire to stand always for the right, to keep before them the dignity of true and honest toil; to teach them to keep themselves sober, temperate and honest; to encourage them to march steadily on with a true determination to work, save and endure; always keeping their mind's eye on the great goal of progress.

The Atlantic Advocate's original staff included Wilfred A. DeCosta, president and assistant editor; George Roache, vice-president; M. F. Jemmott, editor; Miriam A. DeCosta, secretary; and William Thomas, circulation manager. In 1916 the DeCosta's and Dr. Clement Courtney Ligoure incorporated the business as the Atlantic Advocate Association Ltd; Wilfred DeCosta was president, Dr. Ligoure was vice-president, Miriam DeCosta was secretary, William J. and Ella J. Thomas were treasurer and assistant treasurer, respectively, and Ethelbert Lionel Cross was editor. Presumably, Cross resigned because he had enlisted on 2 January, 1917 and had become a sergeant in No. 2 Construction Battalion.

By April 1917, Dr. Ligoure was editor and publisher, Wilfred DeCosta was honorary president, and Miriam DeCosta was secretary.

Below are the biographical sketches of the *Advocate's* staff prepared by Philip Hartling; these are reprinted with the kind permission of Mr. Hartling.

MIRIAM A. DeCOSTA   **WILFRED A. DeCOSTA**

M.A. DeCosta was *The Atlantic Advocate's* secretary from 1915 to 1917 and treasurer in January 1917. Mrs. DeCosta's articles, "The Late J.R. Johnston" and "The Road to Prosperity" appeared in the magazine's first issue.

Wilfred DeCosta was *The Atlantic Advocate's* assistant editor in 1915, president from 1915 to 1917 and honourary president in April and May 1917. He contributed at least two articles to the magazine: "Right Thinking" in April 1915 and "Duty" in January 1917.

DeCosta, who was born in the British West Indies, was living in Halifax by 1908-09 where he was employed as a landscape gardener at the Pearson family estate, "Emscote." The annual *McAlpine's Halifax City Directory* lists his occupations as landscape gardener (1908-09 to 1912), manager of the collection agency, Maritime Mercantile Agency (1913) and gardener (1914-17). Sergeant-Major DeCosta of No. 2 Construction Battalion, is listed in the 1917 directory as being "OAS" (On Active Service).

MOWBRAY FITZGERALD JEMMOTT   **CLEMENT COURTENAY LIGOURE**

M. F. Jemmott was born in Bridgetown, Barbados, where he started his teaching career at St. Mary's Boys' College. He taught in Newfoundland for two years before coming to Nova Scotia to continue his teaching career. Within the province he taught at Lucasville, Hammonds Plains, Preston, and lastly at Africville, where he taught for thirty years before retiring due to ill health in 1933.

Mr. Jemmott married Teresa Esther Clayton of Halifax in 1903. He was *The Atlantic Advocate's* first editor and the magazine's office was located in his residence at 58 Gottingen Street in 1915. When he died at age 66 in 1941, *The Halifax Herald* of 27 January reported that this ex-principal of the Africville School was known as a "walking Encyclopaedia of the Negro Race," because of his extraordinary memory.

Dr. C.C. Ligoure was born in San Fernando, Trinidad on 13 October, 1887. His father, C. F. Ligoure, was Deputy Marshall of the Supreme Court.

Although C. C. Ligoure entered the Faculty of Medicine at Queen's University, Kingston, Ontario, for the 1906-07 session, he left at the end of the academic year 1908-09. However, he returned in 1912, received a MB (Bachelor of Medicine) in September 1914 and a MD in April 1916. By June of the latter year, he was living in a house at "Emscote," Halifax.

Dr. C. C. Ligoure lived at 166 North Street, presently 5812 North Street, from 1917 to 1921. His residence was also the Amanda Private Hospital during these years, and the office of *The Atlantic Advocate* in 1917.

A "Release of Agreement" (cancellation of sale) between Ligoure and Mary R. DeWolfe for the property at 166 North Street was recorded in the Registry of Deeds in February 1921. It would appear that Dr. Ligoure then left Halifax. *The Medical Register...of Nova Scotia...June 30, 1923* noted that Dr. C. C. Ligoure had been "removed by death since last issue of register." The records of the American Medical Association indicate that Dr. Ligoure died in Halifax on 23 May, 1922. However, a search of available records at the Public Archives of Nova Scotia has not confirmed this information.

GEORGE ROACHE

George Roache, son of Robert and Adelaide Roache, was born in Halifax. He operated Roache's Lunch Room, 168 Gottingen Street, which advertised in *The Atlantic Advocate* (April 1915) that it served "Home Made Pastry/Steaks and Chops/Served in a way you'll like/Oysters in all Styles/and the/Best Cup of Coffee in the Ctiy [sic]."

Mr. Roache was the vice-president of the magazine in 1915. After he died at age 55 in 1918, his obituary noted that he "…was a man of great geniality and kindness of heart, whole souled, generous and greatly liked." (*The Evening Mail*, April 18, 1918)."

Twelve years after *The Atlantic Advocate* ceased publication, the first edition of the *Nova Scotia Gleaner* hit the streets in August 1929. Its founder was Frederick Allan Hamilton, who was born in the British West Indies in 1895. From what is known of his early life, Hamilton enrolled at Dalhousie University in 1917 and graduated with BA and LLB degrees. He then moved to Sydney, Cape Breton, in 1922 to practice law at 204 Charlotte Street. In the *Nova Scotia Gleaner*, Hamilton was listed as editor and publisher. The stated object of this monthly publication was to unify "the colored people of the Province of Nova Scotia," possibly by sharing information and activities since there were "Notes" from different parts of the province but no hint of social and political activism.

Hamilton came to Halifax from Scarborough on the island of Tobago in what was then the British West Indies. He was one of five black students from the West Indies at Dalhousie when he had cause to write a letter to the editor of the *Dalhousie Gazette* on March 17, 1918. The letter was in protest against a decision by the students' union in October 1917 barring black students from attending social functions of the university. This was followed by a letter to the *Gazette* written by a white student under the pseudonym "Controlled Democracy" impugning the character of black students. The university president, Dr. A. Stanley Mackenzie intervened. In what terms, the records do not say, but in a letter to the president dated March 12, 1918, the five West Indian students stated that "in the interest of the University, we beg to waive our undeniable right on the question raised by 'Controlled Democracy' and leave our defence entirely in your hands."

Part of what "Controlled Democracy," from Kentville, Nova Scotia, wrote on March 4, 1918, referred to "too many instances of the lamentable results of too free association of the Ethiopian male with the white female…[and] the desire of parents to protect their daughters against it."

Hamilton went on to complete his law degree in 1923 and shortly afterwards married Emma Johnson of Hammonds Plains before moving to Sydney. Their one daughter, Marion, became the director of Cooperative Grocery Stores in Whitney Pier, Sydney. More information on F. Allan Hamilton appears in the chapter on pioneering lawyers. Here his work as the publisher of the *Nova Scotia Gleaner* will be considered.

That Hamilton was thinking of the future of the black community in his endeavours is clear from a speech he delivered at the opening of the Universal Negro Improvement Association Hall at New Waterford as reported in the *Gleaner*'s "New Waterford Notes" on October 5. 1929:

After congratulating the officers and members for conceiving the idea [of build-ing the hall] and putting it into effect, the speaker said that the action showed that we had men who had a vision of the future and men who were looking further than the everyday routine of life, men who were striving to leave something behind them to serve the future hour. He pointed out that although the race is in its infancy we have had several builders in the past, men who have left a monument behind them that the others coming after may see (…Dumas, Toussaint L'Ouverture, Douglas, Dunbar, Washington, Garvey). He further said that this should only be the beginning of greater undertakings and that we should all try to leave some monument behind so that the young ones coming after will see that we have not lived in vain and will try to do at least better than we did.

The hall that Hamilton spoke about was built to honour the work of Marcus Garvey, Jamaican-born black activist. Garvey used the columns of his journal, *The Black Man*, to spread black consciousness in an effort to achieve economic and political redemption. He appointed himself as "emperor" of the black race, and his fiery advocacy spread from Jamaica to the United States and major cities in Canada, reaching New Waterford in 1919.

The *Nova Scotia Gleaner* was similar to *The Atlantic Advocate* in size and for-mat. It was six pages in length and covered news concerning black communities throughout Nova Scotia. Little is known about the *Nova Scotia Gleaner*, except that it was a monthly publication with offices in 204 Charlotte Street, Sydney. Its first issue appeared in August 1929. A single copy cost 10¢ while an annual subscription cost $1.00. The duration of its publication is not known. No men-tion of it has been found in the columns of the *Clarion*.

The third of the pioneering black papers was the *Clarion*, which was first pub-lished in 1945 as a single 8" x 10" sheet, and later expanded as a church bulletin in 1946. Its publisher was Carrie M. Best, born in New Glasgow in 1903, the daughter of James Prevoe and Gordinia (Ashe) Prevoe.

CARRIE BEST, CELEBRATED EDITOR OF THE *CLARION*

After its modest beginning in 1945, the *Clarion* was incorporated as the Clarion Publishing Company Ltd. in 1947, with Lemuel B. Mills, a New Glasgow contractor, and Dr. A. E. Waddell, a prominent Halifax physician from the West Indies, as the company's officers. Carrie Best continued as editor with her son, Calbert James Best, as assistant editor. Calbert Best was perhaps the first black journalist to obtain a diploma in journalism from King's College in Halifax. He later served in the federal public service for almost forty years in senior positions. From 1985 to 1988 Calbert Best served as the Canadian High Commissioner to Trinidad and Tobago.

The *Clarion* grew into a national newspaper, the *Negro Citizen*, in 1949 but ceased publication entirely in 1956, owing to a decline in circulation as other black national papers appeared. In March 1992, the *Clarion* made a re-appearance under the auspices of a new Clarion Publishing Company Limited. The Clarion of 1947 had the motto "For Inter-Racial Understanding and Good Will" while the 1992 incarnation features "Voices of the Visible Minority Past, Present and Future." The two mottoes are an expression of Carrie Best's lived experience, in which she straddled the racial divide with an oratory and a memory that made her one of Nova Scotia's best-known personalities of any colour or creed. Her autobiography, *That Lonesome Road*, published in 1977, tells a remarkable story of her world and her writings.

Founder of the Kay Livingstone Visible Minority Women's Society of Nova Scotia and an officer of the Order of Canada, Carrie M. Best died in New Glasgow on July 24, 2001, at age ninety-seven. The editorial in the *Chronicle Herald* on July 26, 2001, paid well-deserved tribute to this remarkable woman:

Nova Scotia lost a great woman this week with the death in New Glasgow of human rights leader, journalist, author, poet and humanitarian, Dr. Carrie Best.... She was best known as creator and publisher of Nova Scotia Clarion, a newspaper that promoted interracial understanding and investigated racism and discrimination in the province during the 1940s and 50s.... A woman of outstanding worth, a tenacious crusader for good and noble causes, a gracious lady who has devoted her life and her generous gifts to the betterment of the human condition. She has given hope and dignity to her own race and is an example and inspiration to all people in both word and work....

The editor of the *Clarion*, Carrie M. Best, and the associate editor, James Calbert Best, used the paper to denounce racial discrimination in theatres, restaurants, and schools. Almost every issue carried articles with bold headlines: "Will Education Solve the Race Problem?"; "U.N.B. students will Boycott Barbershops. Four Main Shops Alleged to have Discriminated Against Negroes"; "Halifax B.Y.P.U. Holds Discussion on Job Opportunities for Race Members"; "New Glasgow Restaurants Persist in 'Jim Crow'"; "Is This a Free Country?"

VOLUME I

THE CLARION

MARCH 1992

VOICES OF THE VISIBLE MINORITY PAST, PRESENT AND FUTURE

Published by the Clarion Publishing Company Ltd.
599 So. Washington St., New Glasgow, N.S.

ETHICS ★ OWNERSHIP ★ QUALITY

Carrie M. Best, OC., LL.D.
EDITOR AND PUBLISHER

THE VALUE OF THE MEDIA

There are many professions which if applied would give meaning to equality, justice and the shaping of legislation that would guarantee these rights to all regardless of race, creed or color.

Three of these have been given top priority: Church, Education and Politics.

The precepts that direct moral and religious thought should emanate from the pulpit, while the schools and universities reflect a broader intellectual culture.

The field of politics should give us practical experience in the complicated, misinterpreted and often misunderstood science of government (on all levels) and in so doing afford all an opportunity for actual participation in the shaping of legislation, thereby giving meaning and vitality to public policies.

Conceding all due respect to the noble men and women of the past who stood in the vanguard of their missions, the question as to whether or not their descendants are equally as dedicated and assertive is often debated.

THE FIFTH ESTATE

A free and independent press occupies a unique position with reference to all of these in the struggle for the elevation of the masses, as more and more dependence on the press is being noted.

It is the lever to which all our professions must look for support in carrying out their objectives - good or bad.

It is the concentrated voice of the masses and has been referred to as the "Mouthpiece of the Age" and the "Universal Censor", directed by popular opinion, from whose verdict there is no appeal.

It is the mythical yet very real "Court of Public Opinion."

THE CATALYST

A free and independent press is the medium through which the great work of the church universal is disseminated, while the labors of educational leaders are magnified, thus contributing to the growth of intelligence.

Its pages are the text books for those without access to university libraries and its editorial pages often the thesis for graduation into the School of Life.

Politically, the press has long been recognized as an institution more powerful than any individual - evolving over the years from a mere messenger of happenings in a restricted area, to the mastermind in the economy of nations.

LAST STRONGHOLD

At a period in history when long established freedoms are being threatened and institutions designed to protect them (once green and growing) are showing signs of the dry rot of nepotism, the free and independent press may well be the last stronghold of democracy.

Newspapers are feared by tyrants. Napoleon Bonaparte, once remarked with a bitterness born of impending doom, that newspapers were more to be feared than bayonets, and he has fully justified this observation as it relates to 20th Century journalism.

FROM THE EDITOR'S DESK

Sitting at my dining room table one day in 1949, I drafted the first *Clarion* - a very insignificant sheet of paper about six inches square. I was 43 years old. Today, February 14, 1992 as I near my 89th birthday. I am drafting the first of a revised edition of the original *Clarion* that ceased publication in 1956.

My concept of a communication medium designed to meet the needs of minority groups, remains now, as it was then — a totally self-supported *independent* press as outlined in *The Value of the Media* written twenty years later when I was a columnist for the Pictou Advocate.

Consequently, this humble effort is to allow the intelligent, informed and concerned members of a particular group of citizens the opportunity to share their knowledge within an editorial framework as a valuable contribution to Black History on the topics of Church, Education, History, Politics and the Justice System. The *Clarion* extends to all to regard this humble effort as an invitation to contribute.

THE CHURCH

The influence of the Black Church on the progress and achievements of Black Nova Scotians is immeasureable. It has been referred to as a Lighthouse laden with human souls upon the tempestuous sea of hatred and discrimination.

We are indebted to those servants of the church who have constantly admonished their people to embrace thrift to educate their children and enjoined them to be honest, sober, and industrious citizens as a means of survival. Laboring often with "bricks without straw", they have "builded better than they knew".

EDUCATION

The aim or purpose of education is always, has been, and ever will be only a preparation for complete living, enabling the recipient to be useful in one's day and generation.

To secure this, requires the acquisition of knowledge found in the fields of human endeavour.

First, man and his experiences and external nature.

Second, training to intelligent and productive activity in the use of this knowledge and the proper use and enjoyment of it.

Next Issue:

Economics, Politics, History and the Justice System from a Black Perspective.

AN ISSUE OF THE *CLARION*

In the 1947 editorial bearing that last headline, the paper excoriated the racist practices of New Glasgow cinema owners:

In a free country one man is as good as another—any well-behaved person may enter any public place. In Nova Scotia a Negro woman tried to sit in the downstairs section of a theatre instead of the Jim Crow gallery. Not only was she ejected by force but thereafter she, not the theatre owner, was charged and convicted of a misdemeanor.

These are but few examples of the causes that the *Clarion* espoused without fear or favour.

Black pioneers in the press also included printers, such as Ernest Marshall, who is known to have been active in Halifax in the 1940s. While the extent of Marshall's skills and working life are not known to the authors, another pioneering black printer in Halifax went on to become top in his field for almost half a century. He is Arthur Ruck, youngest son of George Ruck of Sydney, and youngest of the Ruck brothers, Winston, Calvin, Lionel, and stepbrother Vernal Braithwaite.

ARTHUR RUCK AT WORK AT THE DARTMOUTH FREE PRESS

Arthur Ruck learnt printing through private correspondence courses offered by the International Telegraphic Union in the early 1950s, after having completed high school at Sydney Academy. He came to Halifax at age twenty-two, where he attended part-time courses at Saint Mary's University at night, and worked at the Dartmouth Free Press, located first on Ochterloney Street in 1954 and later on Wyse Road after 1959. By then Ruck was foreman of the plant—a rare position for a black man at the time. He worked at the Dartmouth Free Press for fifteen years before moving on in 1969 to MT&T, where he served for twenty-five years, rising to the position of systems manager at the print shop on Joseph Howe Drive, another position of responsibility. He retired in 1994.

In an interview at his house in Halifax in 2004, Arthur Ruck recalled incidents and highlights from his long career. On one occasion, he was invited over the phone to start working the following day for the *Chronicle Herald*. When he turned up with his lunch bag in hand he was made to wait and wait until he raised the matter himself, only to be told that the white workers would not welcome a black colleague. On another occasion, he attended a three-week workshop in Chicago, where one of the courses was run by Bill Gates. Gates offered Ruck a job in the United States, whereupon Ruck replied, "You come to Canada and I will work for you." In Ruck's estimation, Bill Gates was a good man who knew his job. For a pioneer who suffered from poor health for most of his life and who worked long and hard to excel in his field, Arthur Ruck certainly knew his job, too.

Chapter 5

Pioneering Lawyers

JAMES ROBINSON JOHNSTON

Pioneers in the legal profession came after the pastors and the teachers had begun their work to provide leadership in the black communities. The preparation needed to enter the profession was long and costly, requiring both family and community support during difficult economic times. As society developed, the need for lawyers to guide and protect the needy became more pressing; at the same time, West Indian immigrants began arriving in Canadian universities to take up higher studies. To many, the legal profession had always been a tantalizing one: so many aspired to enter it, so few actually got in—but those who did made their mark as visionaries of change. It is believed that

Robert Sutherland, who was born in Jamaica in 1830 when slavery still existed, was the first black lawyer in Canada. He entered Queen's University in Kingston, Ontario, in 1849, after a few years of high school study in Kingston. He went on to study law at Osgoode Hall, was called to the bar in 1852, and practised in Walkerton until he died young in 1878. He left his entire estate to Queen's University on whose grounds a tombstone stands today in memory of this gift.

Prior to the appearance on the Nova Scotia scene of lawyer James Robinson Johnston, whose life and work bear some poignant parallels to that of Robert Sutherland, the only black lawyer in the Maritimes was Abraham B. Walker, who was born in British Columbia and studied law in the United States before moving to New Brunswick in 1890. In 1903 he founded a journal called *Neith*, in whose columns he advocated black advancement through sustained education in every branch of learning: science, literature, philosophy, religion, politics, journalism, and the law.

James R. Johnston was born in 1876. He started his schooling at Maynard Street School for Negro Boys in 1882. Two years later the school was amalgamated with the Lockman Street School for Negro Girls. As the amalgamated school expanded, it relocated to the North End Mission. In these years the general social environment in Halifax was laden with racism. Segregated black settlements were everywhere; segregated black schools were common; discrimination in hiring practices and in housing was the norm. For the most part, Nova Scotia was a racist society in line with the Canadian, not the American, model of racism: it was covert, not overt; it was mostly not buttressed by law, but it existed and it was hurtful.

Fortunately for James Johnston, the new principal at the North End Mission, Jane Bruce, was one of those rare people who were willing to look beyond the colour barrier; she recognized Johnston's special character and intelligence. On her recommendation, he was transferred to the Halifax Academy in 1887. In 1892 he entered Dalhousie University, where he earned a BA in literature in 1896 and an LLB in 1898.

These accomplishments are especially remarkable in light of the difficulties facing black students. They mostly attended separate schools, which were at first supported only by missionary societies and churches; these schools were staffed by black teachers, who were hard to find and who had poor schooling themselves. In many settlements, schools for black children were closed for months and years at a time. After 1808, government school subsidies were available to areas with at least thirty families who held land in freehold, built a school house, hired a teacher, and raised between £50 and £200—clearly conditions that black communities could not meet. All the black teachers of the day had left for Sierra Leone in 1792. There were only three black teachers on record in the early decades following the arrival of the Black Refugees in 1813: Thomas Brownpriggs, Dempsey Jordan, and John Pleasant. The lack of resources, teachers, spaces, and funds, along with the rigours of the "colour line," explain how detrimental the situation was and why William S. Fielding, managing editor of the *Halifax Morning Chronicle* would say in 1884 in the debate on whether or not to provide permanent segregated schooling that laws were made "for the greatest good of the greatest number," and that "many negroes were satisfied and wished to have separate schools," and that white "parents would send their children to private schools rather than permit racial mixing."

In the end a compromise was struck: the Education Act of 1884 (reaffirmed in 1918) stated that a black child could not be excluded from attending a school in the ward or section in which the child resided. At the same time, government would continue to provide for separate schools for gender and race. Black students were not admitted to the Provincial Normal College until 1918. It was only in 1954 that all references to race were dropped from the Education Act.

James R. Johnston had a vision for black youth, which was centred round an important educational aim: the provision of accessible higher education. This can be seen in his proposal for setting up a Normal and Industrial Institute—a proposal which found a place after his death in the formation of the Nova Scotia Home for Coloured Children in 1921.

Johnston's LLB graduating class of 1898 comprised twenty-five graduates. In the *Dalhousie Gazette* of October 26, 1898, the following remarks are made on Johnston:

He will, we understand, put out his shingles in Halifax. He deserves great credit for the admirable way he has overcome obstacles to obtain a thorough preparation for the bar, and no doubt his untiring efforts will secure for him a prominent place in the future of our country.

JAMES R. JOHNSTON'S NAME PLATE

James R. Johnston did hang out his shingles, at 197 Hollis Street, opposite the Provincial Building, and ten years later, closer to the heart of the legal community at 58 Bedford Row, which he shared with George Ritchie, who had lectured in law during Johnston's years as a student. In spite of the difficulties for black students wishing to obtain access to education in Johnston's day, and the existence of the "colour line," he got into law school; made the passing grade; articled with the firm of Russell and Russell, whose senior partner, Benjamin Russell, was professor and secretary of the Faculty of Law; and became the partner of Ritchie, a Harvard graduate and his former professor. All these achievements show the measure of the man, his intellect, and his personality.

Over the years he provided legal services to many clients in need, including a drug addict in a police court, black men on rape charges, a quartermaster on charges of irregularities, and black employees on the railway on charges of theft.

There was also a political side to Johnston's life, which is not as well known. In her article about Johnston for the April 1915 issue of *The Atlantic Advocate*, Miriam DeCosta called him "the Conservative leader of his people." There was the example of Abraham Beverley Walker before him who, between 1882 and 1900, had worked strenuously in support of the Conservative Party. There would be the similar case, less than a century later, of lawyer Donald H. Oliver. And James Johnston's younger brother, Clarence H. Johnston (1982–1973) also became involved in politics, starting at the age of twenty-three, when he wrote a letter to the prime minister. These were bold efforts in a difficult age. In becoming involved in politics, these did much for the advancement of African Nova Scotians.

James Johnston was also a leader of the Cornwallis Street Baptist church; among other things, he was instrumental in raising nearly $6,000 to pay off the old mortgage and renovate the church in 1914.

Sadly, James Johnton suffered a tragic and early death on March 3, 1915, when he was killed by his wife's brother in a family quarrel. The James Robinson Johnston Endowed Chair in Black Canadian Studies at Dalhousie University in 1992—and the appointment of the first Chair in 1994—recognized his stature and his historical importance. And, of course, his work in the Baptist Young People's Union and the AUBA has always been recalled by these organizations.

Some years after James R. Johnston, Frederick Allan Hamilton, mentioned earlier as the founder of the *Nova Scotia Gleaner*, appeared on the legal scene in 1929. In the *Dalhousie Gazette's* graduation issue for 1923 the following entry appears under Frederick Allan Hamilton, BA:

A student of ability and one of the most consistent case hunters in his year, this Dalhousie graduate in Arts well earned his degree. He was also noted for his ability to ask his professors more questions in shorter time than the majority of his classmates. Hamilton called Scarborough, Tobago, B.W.I., his home.

In the *Halifax Chronicle* of February 2, 1950, a picture of Hamilton appeared when, along with thirteen other Nova Scotian lawyers, he was awarded the title of King's Counsel (KC). The article states that Hamilton, "who has been practising law in Sydney since 1922, is Canada's only Negro King's Counsel." His age was given as fifty-five. He died in Sydney the following year on July 4, 1951.

The third African Nova Scotian who has a place among the pioneering lawyers is George Webber Roache Davis (1925–2004). George Davis, after James R. Johnston, was the second Nova Scotia-born black lawyer. His scholastic achievements as one of the few black students pursuing higher studies need to be told. Born in Halifax, George Davis attended Alexandra School and Queen Elizabeth High School, from which he graduated in 1945. He then enrolled at Dalhousie University and graduated with a BA in 1948. He proceeded to Dalhousie Law School and graduated in 1951. He articled with McInnes, Cooper, Robertson, and started his own practice on Gottingen Street, then a bustling commercial area with flourishing businesses and several banks. Additionally, as George Davis pointed out in an interview on April 14, 1989, there was a vibrant black community in close proximity to his practice.

Not long after George Davis started his law practice in what was then 290 Gottingen Street, he entered into a partnership with Cecil Moore in the same building which lasted until their retirements in the 1980s. In an interview in 2004, Cecil Moore, then eighty-three, described his former partner, who died on April 22, 2004, as a "good friend, of impeccable character who didn't fool around with the truth."

George Davis served a term as registrar of joint stock companies and also served as a member of the Nova Scotia Human Rights Commission and the Housing Commission. He was appointed QC in 1967. He also twice ran for alderman of Ward 5.

As a member of the North End Halifax black community, George Davis was a participant and leader in many of the community's social, cultural, and political activities. He was also a key member of the Nova Scotia Association for the Advancement of Coloured People in its early years. In all these positions, George Davis was breaking new ground. He was, in a way, preparing the path for others, like Donald Oliver, who were to follow.

GEORGE WEBBER DAVIS

F.A. HAMILTON

DONALD H. OLIVER,
LAWYER AND
SENATOR

The next pioneering lawyer in this section is Donald Oliver, who was born in Wolfville, Nova Scotia, in 1938. He graduated with a BA with honours in history from Acadia University in 1960 and was class valedictorian. He then enrolled at the Dalhousie University Law School, graduating in 1964 with an LLB plus many prizes: the Sir James Dunn Scholarship in Law, the G. O. Forsythe Prize for Scholarship and Character, and the Faculty of Law Scholarship. Donald Oliver began practising in Halifax in 1965 at Stewart McKelvey Stirling Scales and also taught law for many years at Dalhousie University, the Technical University of Nova Scotia, and Saint Mary's University. The contribution of Donald H. Oliver, QC, to community life, social causes, and political life is remarkably long, dedicated, and distinguished. Besides being a lawyer and politician, Oliver served for many years as chair of the Halifax Children's Aid Society, the Metro Volunteer Resource Centre, the Black Cultural Society, and the Black United Front, and as governor of the Technical University of Nova Scotia. He was appointed to the Canadian senate on September 7, 1990. Before that he had served for two terms as national vice-president of the Conservative Party of Canada–Atlantic Region.

The pioneering few discussed in this chapter walked a lonely and difficult path in their day, but they left a legacy that was picked up by the later graduates and practitioners, of whom they—and the province and country—would be proud. Though the list is far from complete, taken together, it is impressive and promising. The long-standing "colour line" still exists, though it is fading by the decade, sometimes too slowly, but fading it is, as more and more black youth appear on the scene, diversify their expertise, and climb the rungs of their chosen ladder. There are many later lawyers deserving of recognition here:

- **WAYNE KELSIE** (LLB, 1972)

- **ANTHONY ROSS** (LLB, 1973)

- **HOBARTSON AUGUSTUS JAMES (GUS) WEDDERBURN** (LLB, 1973), is a highly personable public figure who will be discussed later in relation to his teaching career, as well as his involvement with the Nova Scotia Association for the Advancement of Coloured People, and the Black Cultural Society

- **KEN CRAWFORD** (LLB, 1975), who was appointed QC in 1997

- **CASTOR WILLIAMS** (LLB, 1976), appointed to the bench as provincial court judge in Nova Scotia in 1996

- **DOUGLAS RUCK** (LLB, 1977), who served as ombudsman for Nova Scotia for five years and is now vice-chair of the Canada Industrial Relations Board

- **CORRINE SPARKS** (LLB, 1979), first African Nova Scotian to be appointed to the bench in 1987 and Canada's first black woman judge

- **DURNLEY (ROCKY) JONES** (LLB, 1992), first law graduate of the Indigenous Black and Mi'kmaq Programme at the Dalhousie Law School, and recipient of the honorary degree of Doctor of Laws from Guelph University in 2004

- **VALERIE MILLER** (LLB, 1985), who articled with the Federal Department of Justice, specializing in tax litigation, was appointed QC in 2002 (the first black Nova Scotian woman to receive this appointment), and is currently the director of tax law services for the Department of Justice in the Atlantic region.

- **MICHELLE WILLIAMS** (LLM, 2001), served as policy advisor to the Federal Minister of State for Multiculturalism and Status of Women, and is currently Assistant Professor and Director of the Indigenous Black and Mi'kmaq Programme at Dalhousie Law School.

H. A. J.
WEDDERBURN

KEN CRAWFORD

DOUGLAS RUCK

CORRINE SPARKS

MICHELLE WILLIAMS

Chapter 6

Pioneering Lay Personalities and Secular Organizations:
A Century Considered, 1885-1985

**HALIFAX COLORED CITIZENS IMPROVEMENT LEAGUE
PICNIC AT FRANKLYN PARK**

The secular and spiritual sides of the Nova Scotia black experience have always coexisted, complementing and reinforcing each other. This chapter highlights the secular side of this relationship.

PETER EVANDER MCKERROW

Peter Evander McKerrow, clerk and secretary-treasurer of the African United Baptist Association, from 1876–1906, deserves pride of place as a layperson whose contribution to the black Baptist churches was perhaps as profound as that of the ordained pastors. In his thirty years in office, he came to know the work of the churches, their history, and their personalities. He was also an accomplished researcher and writer. His book, *A Brief History of the Coloured Baptists of Nova Scotia and their First Organization as Churches, A.D. 1832*, first published in 1895, is a pioneering and seminal publication that later authors and generations have used extensively.

Peter McKerrow was born in Antigua, British West Indies, on February 23, 1841, and came to Nova Scotia some twenty-one years later. In 1863 he married Mary Eliza Thomas, the eldest daughter of the pastor of the Cornwallis Street Baptist Church and moderator of the AUBA, Rev. James Thomas, a white pastor. This gave McKerrow an opportunity to advance his policy of integrating with the white church, which never caught on, as Pearleen Oliver explains in her *Brief History of the Colored Baptists of Nova Scotia*:

> *His motion to dissolve the Association was made in good faith. Being a man ahead of his times, he felt our union with the white Baptists to be both Christian and expedient. However, he never forced his will upon the people and allowed them to ponder and decide.... When the people decided against the dissolution, McKerrow plunged in again and guided the organization over the threshold of the twentieth century.*
>
> *We honour him for the excellent records he left for us; we honour him for the interest he, a stranger, took in our people, and we honour him for his sterling character.*

Peter McKerrow died on December 22, 1906. His position as clerk of the AUBA was taken over by his nephew, James R. Johnston.

James Johnston's brother, Clarence H. Johnston, followed successfully in the distinguished family footsteps and was first appointed superintendent of the Cornwallis Street Baptist Church Sunday school in 1913, a position which he held for more than thirty-five years. During his long service to Cornwallis Street Baptist Church he was also senior deacon and chairman of the board of trustees. He was also a charter member and founder of the Equity Masonic Lodge.

His daughter, Aleta Williams, and son, Noel Johnston, were both distinguished contributors to the Nova Scotia black community in journalism, religion, community development, and education. Aleta Williams was educated in Halifax. She held various positions in the Cornwallis Street Baptist Church, including organist, choir director, and Sunday school teacher. She married Albert Murray Williams, and brought up seven children while holding many positions in the service of church and community. She was a founding member of the Pictou County YM-YWCA and the Inter-Racial Council, and a board member of the Aberdeen Hospital, the Black United Front, and the Nova Scotia Seniors Secretariat. She also worked for the *New Glasgow Evening News* in various positions. Her brother, Noel Johnston, was a long-serving teacher and a board member of the Black Cultural Society.

Clarence H. Johnston died on November 30, 1973 at the age of 81.

JAMES A. R. KINNEY AND THE FORMATION OF THE NOVA SCOTIA HOME FOR COLOURED CHILDREN

When James R. Johnston died on March 3, 1915, there was a vacuum in the financial leadership of the church. It was in this context, according to C. H. Johnston, that "James A. R. Kinney was invited to take an active part in the work of the church." This invitation brought into the limelight a prominent personality whose name became synonymous with the birth and growth of the Nova Scotia Home for Coloured Children. Born in Yarmouth, Nova Scotia, in 1878, James A. R. Kinney was the first black graduate of the Maritime Business College in 1897. He worked for twenty-six years as advertising manager for William Stairs, Son and Morrow Company, which was first located in Sackville, near Halifax, and later moved to Halifax at a location on Strawberry Hill. At the same time, except for a brief interval, Kinney was a leading member of the AUBA as clerk and treasurer. It was this affiliation that connected him to the Nova Scotia Home for Coloured Children.

As early as 1900, officers of the AUBA had started discussions on the need for an institution to take care of disadvantaged and orphaned children in the black community. It was James R. Johnston, holder of the influential position of clerk of the AUBA in 1906, who became well placed to advance a proposal he had drafted a year earlier for the establishment of a normal and industrial school. He saw this as a way to break down the prejudice that existed in rural black communities against post-secondary education. Supported by the pastor of the Cornwallis Street Baptist Church, Rev. Moses B. Puryear, the scheme was endorsed by civic and church leaders in 1914. Clearly, the need for a multi-purpose institution was timely: in 1913-14 three cases were well documented of motherless black babies with no place to go because of the pervasive colour prejudices of the day.

In September 1915, in the midst of the emotionally charged mourning period following the death of James R. Johnston, the Johnston-Puryear proposal was adopted by the AUBA, and a committee was struck to take the matter forward. The AUBA's resolution of September 1915, made the following statement:

> *WHEREAS there is no institution for the Industrial, Domestic and Business training of our young men and women;*
> *AND WHEREAS it is the duty of the Race to produce its own leaders who shall be architects to carve our place in Western Civilization;*
> *THEREFORE BE IT RESOLVED that we, the African United Baptist Association, endorse, by moral and financial aid, the proposed institution to be known as the Industrial School of Nova Scotia for Coloured Children.*

Two years later, the first board of trustees was appointed, an interracial one, with Henry G. Bauld as president, R. H. Murray as secretary, and G. R. Hart as treasurer. The other board members were Rev. Moses Puryear, Ernest H. Blois, C. Strickland, Charles Coleman Blackadar, John Murphy, Thomas P. Johnson and J. A. R. Kinney. This was indeed a formidable team: Blackadar owned the *Acadian Recorder*; Murphy and Strickland were bank managers; Blois had been Superintendent of the Halifax Industrial School (1906) and in 1912 was appointed superintendent of Neglected and Dependent Children, and years later became deputy minister of social services; Johnson was the county councillor for Preston; and Kinney, as mentioned above, was the advertising manager for William Stairs, Son and Morrow. Henry Gibson Bauld, a prominent businessman in wholesale trade, was devoted to the cause and went on to serve as president of the home from its opening in 1921 until his death on February 4, 1948.

The industrial school had a short life. Following a public appeal in October 1917 by the above-named board of trustees, three of whose members were from the black community, the sum of $1,500 was raised. The City of Halifax donated $500, the firm for which Kinney worked donated $100, and a black businessman and restaurant owner in Halifax, George Roache, donated $25. A building was acquired on Quinpool Road in Halifax and was renovated and equipped to accommodate the industrial school and the students who needed accommodation. Julia Jackson was recruited as matron from Philadelphia. The matron assumed office on November 15, 1917. The Halifax Explosion on December 6, 1917 changed the project's initial premises and scope, but the dream for its realization lived on.

There were three pillars to this dream: industrial, domestic, and business. James A. R. Kinney, one of the three original black trustees of the project, embodied these three pillars in his life, experience, and vision. He was the connecting link between the nine trustees left in the post–Halifax Explosion era (1917–21) and the black church and community. Together, they began looking for a new site where they could start afresh. A 211-acre site in Westphal, known as the McKenzie property, was purchased with government assistance, and a building was erected. The AUBA annual convention was informed in September 1920, in the following words:

We are exceedingly pleased to bring to the attention of the Association that the beautiful building which is to house the Nova Scotia Orphan and Neglected Children is now under construction, some $40,000 having been raised.... It is a home of great possibilities for the Race and from it can emerge those fitting for training which will enable them to pursue higher educational branches, and lay a foundation for leadership of the Race....

These were clearly Kinney's words. He wanted the AUBA and its affiliates to support the venture on an ongoing basis with an amount of some $2,000 annually. "If we fail in this means of support, we will lose out in the great essentials of racial opportunity which the Government and our friends have seen fit to provide," the report concluded.

The Nova Scotia Home for Coloured Children was officially opened on June 6, 1921, under a board of directors headed by Henry G. Bauld, who served until his death in 1969. The first black president of the home was Dr. Donald E. Fairfax, who assumed office in 1974 and served for three terms. James A. R. Kinney served as secretary-treasurer of the board and superintendent of the home from 1921 until his death in 1940. They were all distinguished pioneers of a secular institution rooted in black history, aspirations, and initiatives.

The home operated as a foster home, a school, and a farm. In most years it provided accommodation for an average of forty children. The school curriculum was in accordance with provincial government standards, and the teachers were inspected from time to time. The children did light work on the farm, such as picking crops.

There were other pioneers associated with the home, such as Muriel States, who was only thirty-seven when her husband, Rev. Wellington States, died in 1927, and who joined the home in 1931 to serve as supervisor of children. Others associated with the home include the first three matrons, Martha G. Harris, Sadie Steen, and Elizabeth A. Fowler (the first African Nova Scotian matron); the earliest teachers, Gladys Walcott (1921–30), Portia White (1931), and the Morgan sisters, Joyce and Shirley; and James Bundy from nearby Cherrybrook, who worked at the home in various positions for forty-three years starting in 1921.

When the Henry G. Bauld two-room school opened at the home in June 1948 as a memorial to the institution's first president, another link to the past appeared in the person of Patricia Riley, the daughter of Rev. Wellington States and Muriel States. She and Iva Clayton were the first two instructors at this new school.

James A. R. Kinney had spoken in his report of 1920 of the great possibilities that lay ahead for the resident children at the home to pursue higher education and take their place in leadership roles in the future. While it will be some time before a fuller picture emerges, Charles R. Saunders provides a preliminary appraisal of the home's success in *Share and Care: The Story of the Nova Scotia Home for Colored Children*:

Although the majority of the children from the Home became manual labourers or domestics, some of Mrs. Riley's pupils achieved greater success. One, who we'll call "Christopher Robinson" became the first resident of the NSHCC to graduate from high school. He later attended Saint Mary's University in Halifax and became an accountant. Joyce Davidson went on to become a stenographer, and Wayne Kelsie was called to the bar as an attorney. Other students of Mrs. Riley became nurses and secretaries, and many occupied prominent positions in the black community....

THE NEW NSHCC, OPENED IN 1978

This volume cannot attempt to give a detailed account of the home beyond the early decades. But some notable highlights are in order. In 1978, the home moved to new premises nearby. Since 1974 a succession of black presidents have steered the institution: Rev. D. E. Fairfax, Wayne Kelsie, Gertrude Tynes, James Francois, and Bryan Darrell. The last white executive director, Robert Butler, appointed in 1973, was replaced by Wilfred Jackson. As James Francois maintained in his report to the AUBA in 1987,

> *Throughout its history the Home has reflected the changes in society. The closure of large orphanages, the establishment of the Children's Services Act, the shifts in education, the humaneness of the community, the new Young Offenders Act…have all impacted on the NS Home for Colored Children, and have been instrumental to the movement of this Home to its newer facilities and its service to a smaller population.*

WILFRED JACKSON, EXECUTIVE DIRECTOR OF THE NSHCC

The James R. Johnston–Moses Puryear vision of 1905–06 became a reality after an uneven journey, which, along the way, produced pioneering stalwarts, white and black, men and women, religious and secular—many of whom, though not all, have found a place in this volume.

BERESFORD AUGUSTUS HUSBANDS, BUSINESSMAN AND FOUNDER OF THE HALIFAX COLORED CITIZENS IMPROVEMENT LEAGUE

In the early twentieth century, the number of prominent professionals and businessmen from the West Indies living in Halifax was quite high. Following in the footsteps of Dr. Courtney Ligoure and lawyer F. Allan Hamilton came B.

A. Husbands, Dr. F. B. Holder, Dr. A. Calder, and Dr. A. E. Waddell. If anything caused them to stand out, it was their education and their commitment to advancing that of their fellow Nova Scotian citizens. While they were all recognized for the services they rendered, all had to deal with challenges on account of their foreign origins.

One of the most prominent of the West Indian pioneers was Beresford Augustus Husbands, who founded the Halifax Colored Citizens Improvement League, an early secular organization. It was established in Halifax in 1932 and for over a decade was the only organization representing the sizeable black population in the city in social, cultural, economic, and political issues. Led by Husbands from 1932 until his death on June 19, 1968, it loomed large in the life of the city in general and of the black population in particular. Husbands had a varied and interesting life. In his youth he worked for a white Halifax merchant, H. R. Silver; he then moved on to develop his own real estate business, start an important wholesale business, and open a fruit and vegetable store.

Husbands was born in Christ Church, Barbados, in 1883. In 1900 he immigrated to Halifax, where he attended the Joseph Howe School. He later married Iris Lucas of Lucasville, Nova Scotia, with whom he had eight sons and seven daughters. The family house was located on Charles Street in Halifax. Over the years, surviving family members lived in Halifax, Montreal, and Boston. Iris Husbands survived her husband for nine years and died in January 1977 at age ninety-three.

Husbands spared no effort in condemning the injustices of his day: derogatory references to blacks in school texts, discrimination against the training and admission of black nurses, lack of cultural and recreational centres for black youth, barriers in educational and employment opportunities for blacks, and much more. He also sponsored bantam league black hockey teams, helped establish a summer camp for under-privileged children in Lucasville, provided services to black troops calling at the port of Halifax during World War II, and represented the black presence in city parades.

THE HCCIL PARADE FLOAT, 1966

To achieve all this he had divisions within the organization comprising leading citizens of the day, organized under project designations: Halifax North Cultural and Recreation Youth Centre, Colored Men's Conservative Social and Athletic Club, a women's auxiliary committee, and a recreation and entertainment committee.

For all of this, many generations of citizens remembered Beresford Augustus Husbands fondly. The British government awarded him the Order of the British Empire. On August 7, 1982, he was named to the "Wall of Fame" in Halifax, the plaque on which read, "Presented by the city of Halifax in memory of the late Beresford A. Husbands in recognition and appreciation of the outstanding contribution to the advancement of members of the black community of Halifax and thereby of a whole and grateful city."

Following the birth of the Halifax Colored Citizens Improvement League in 1932 came the Halifax Colored Education Centre, founded in 1938 by Dr. F. B. Holder, a West Indian physician who lived and practiced on Maynard Street.

The story of Dr. Alfred E. Waddell is an example of the challenges faced by many West Indians in Halifax. Until the appearance of a television documentary on his life in 2001, his prominence in the black community was not widely recognized, even though he supported black causes (such as those taken up by the NSAACP), supported the publication of the *Clarion* newspaper, advocated justice for Viola Desmond in the New Glasgow segregated cinema case, and made house calls as a physician, not only in Halifax, but as far afield as Hammonds Plains.

Waddell was born in Trinidad in 1896 and emigrated with his wife, Amelia, to New York in 1923, where he put himself through university through night studies. Soon after, he came to Dalhousie University to study medicine. A copy of a reference from the registrar of the Provincial Medical Board of Nova Scotia dated September 15, 1933, testifies that Dr. Alfred E. Waddell graduated with the degrees of Doctor of Medicine and Master of Surgery from Dalhousie University in May 1933, and obtained a licence to practice in Nova Scotia and in Great Britain. The testimonial from Dr. H. L. Scammell ends with the following words: "Dr. Waddell was an excellent student, is a man of fine character and will fill with credit any professional position he may be granted."

Like Beresford Husbands, Dr. Waddell had a keen interest in local and international affairs. In the turbulent years of the thirties leading up to World War II, this was understandable in a port city like Halifax. What was not understandable to those who were well placed and highly educated was the extent of the discrimination practised on both sides of the colour line. Dr. Waddell, like many West Indian immigrants, found that he was shunned by the black community because of his foreign origins and simultaneously shunned by the white community because of his skin colour. It is not surprising that he gravitated towards the Chinese community, small as it was, which welcomed him.

Dr. Waddell had other difficulties to surmount: after graduation from medical school he was denied internship on the racist grounds that white patients would resist treatment by a black doctor. This was only overcome when his class of white students threatened to boycott their own internships in protest. The immigration hurdle was equally daunting, as he had great difficulty with his application to bring his wife and children to join him in Halifax. Yet he persisted, and served society and his patients well.

He made house calls to patients in Africville, Hammonds Plains, Preston, and other black communities. In the Viola Desmond case, the publicity of the time and since has ignored Dr. Waddell's persistent support for the victim during the court case and for years after the conviction. Viola Desmond was arrested on November 8, 1946, in the Roseland Theatre in New Glasgow for sitting downstairs instead of in the balcony reserved for blacks. She spent twelve hours in jail and was charged the following day for attempting to defraud the federal government of 1¢ in amusement tax. (The amusement tax was 3¢ downstairs and 2¢ upstairs). She had a choice between a fine of $20 or a prison term of thirty days. In a series of letters, Dr. Waddell took up this matter of obvious racial discrimination.

To understand Dr. Waddell's convictions and philosophy, one could go back more than ten years before the Viola Desmond case to 1935, when Italy invaded Ethiopia. In a letter to the Halifax *Chronicle-Herald*, dated November 8, 1935, he wrote:

> The Italo-Ethiopian situation is not as complicated as it appears superficially.
> The Western nations, ever altruistic, have dedicated themselves to the sacred mission of "Christianizing" and "civilizing" the African people, and their mission must be carried out, even if, as a by-product, it involves their mass extinction.
> The blacks must be brought by fair, foul or forceful means to believe in a Christianity that preaches brotherhood and practises discrimination; in the civilization that boasts institutions but enforces spectroscopic limitations.
> Meanwhile in the case of the crisis, the World's Star Debating Society continues to make benign resolutions as Italy marches on her crusade of "peaceful penetration."
> Our slogan, amended since 1914, now reads, "Might is Right and White is Might."

Dr. Waddell died on March 20, 1953.

In this brief account of the Caribbean influence on politics and society in Nova Scotia, the name of Henry Sylvester Williams must be included. A Trinidadian, he arrived in Halifax in 1893 at the age of twenty-four and enrolled at Dalhousie University Law School, making him the first black student to enroll in that law school. However, by 1896, he had left and the reasons were not quite clear. According to Barry Cahill, in a newspaper article of 1999, "Why or exactly when Williams left Dalhousie and Nova Scotia remains unclear. Racial harassment may have played its part, for on one occasion he is known to have been assaulted in the law library by a fellow student."

In their recent book *Black Ice*, George and Darril Fosty maintain that Williams established a warm rapport with members of Halifax's black community during his short stay, through attendance at the Cornwallis Street Baptist Church, residence on Gottingen Street, interest in music and politics, friendship and association with James R. Johnston and James A. R. Kinney, and a prominent role in the promotion of two hockey teams, Halifax Eurekas and Halifax Stanley, which were forerunners of the Colored Hockey League. Since both Williams and Johnston were students for a time at Dalhousie, the Fostys speculate,

> Since both men were attending Dalhousie at the same time, it appears logical to assume that Johnston had been among the first to be introduced to Williams upon his arrival in Halifax.... Johnston, in all likelihood, had served as the go-between introducing Williams to the Cornwallis Street Baptist Church and J. A. R. Kinney. We know that Johnston and Williams loved to sing and play the piano during church services and again it appears likely that both participated together during weekend services.

THE NOVA SCOTIA ASSOCIATION FOR THE ADVANCEMENT OF COLOURED PEOPLE

In 1900 Sylvester Williams went on to spearhead the Pan-Africanist Movement, a movement to create continental unity in Africa. It was the forerunner of the National Association for the Advancement of Colored People, which was founded in the United States in 1905 and which in turn influenced the formation of a similar Canadian body in 1924 and a Nova Scotian counterpart in 1945. In these attempts to create black unity and foster black advancement, there is no denying the influence and legacy of the West Indian immigrants discussed above.

Dr. F. B. Holder, a medical doctor from British Guyana, founded the Halifax Colored Education Centre in 1938, helped by some twenty city residents. It served the same constituents and the same geographical area as Beresford A. Husband's Colored Citizens Improvement League, which had been established six years earlier. Public support for both continued and expanded to such an extent that it appeared necessary to form a new and unified organization. A public meeting was held on January 7, 1945, where a constitution committee was struck to consider renaming the Colored Education Centre. On January 28, 1945, a new constitution and a new name were presented and adopted. The Nova Scotia Association for the Advancement of Coloured People was born, incorporated by statute on March 29, 1945. The statute listed the following founding members: Arnold F. Smith, railway employee; Richard Symonds, deacon at Cornwallis Street; William Carter; Bernice Williams, school teacher; Carl Oliver, tradesman; Walter Johnson, instructor at the Nova Scotia Home for Coloured Children; and Ernest Grosse, railway employee. The chairman was Arnold Smith and the secretary was Bernice Williams. The four objectives of the organization were to improve the interests of the coloured people of the province, to encourage and promote fraternity among its members, to cooperate with government and private agencies, and to improve the educational opportunities of colored youth. Summarized in operational terms, the objectives related to education, employment, housing, and human relations.

The two earlier organizations, the Colored Citizens Improvement League and the Colored Education Centre, gave their support to the NSAACP. When the Cornwallis Street Baptist Church, under the leadership of Rev. William P. Oliver, began to give active support, it was but a natural evolution, as almost all the members of the existing organizations were also active members of that church. When both Rev. Oliver and his wife, Pearleen, attended meetings of the NSAACP and championed its causes through the pulpit and public platforms, the combination of spiritual and secular present a formidable challenge to the discriminatory practices faced by the black community.

There was also the necessary camaraderie generated by a strong social club, the Criterion Club, which had been founded in 1936. Its members were the who's who of black Halifax in the thirties and forties, and they included most of the men and women who belonged to the organizations mentioned in these pages.

**CRITERION CLUB,
1942**

These men and women articulated the African Nova Scotian aspirations of their times, long before the civil rights movement in the United States cast its shadow on Canadian soil, long before the 1960s when the re-emergence of Africa created a new pride throughout the African diaspora. Their story is one of confident, contributing, and competent people, going about their work even though relegated to the backwoods of the social order by those who never really made the effort to know them as fellow human beings and who judged them, to use Martin Luther King Jr.'s words, by the colour of their skin and not by the content of their character. In 1995 the NSAACP ceased to exist, having served its time as best it could.

The first high profile challenge for the NSAACP was the Viola Desmond case referred to earlier. Public meetings were held. Carrie Best's *Clarion* newspaper, with its base in New Glasgow where the Roseland Theatre was located, used its column to publicize the injustice surrounding the case, drawing attention to the racial bigotry so rampant in the province in general and New Glasgow in particular. Because of an unfortunate legal oversight, no appeal was lodged within the period allowed, meaning that the Nova Scotia Supreme Court could not consider the request to overturn the decision of the lower court that had convicted Desmond. However, the presiding judge did admit that the real motive in the case against Desmond was "a surreptitious endeavour to enforce a Jim Crow rule through a misuse of a Public Statute." While the NSAACP, its executive, and the *Clarion* publicized the sheer iniquity widely and publicly, others like Dr. Waddell worked behind the scene, as noted earlier. Mrs. Viola Desmond was never legally cleared of the conviction, but the moral victory belonged to her and all the thousands who championed her cause—locally, nationally, and internationally. Nova Scotia politics and society could never be the same again.

At this point, the NSAACP was at its zenith. It was the only black organization between 1945 and the late 1960s to represent the African Nova Scotian community in a broad political context. It engaged with a wide range of issues, including discriminatory practices in schools and workplaces, fair employment and housing practices, human rights, and social justice issues. Though more conciliatory than militant or aggressive in its strategies, it made its case fairly and effectively. It responded to the challenges and opportunities of its time with its available membership and resources. Those who led the organization during its fifty years of existence deserve special mention: Arnold F. Smith (1945–47), Richard S. Symonds (1947–50), Charles Wilson (1950–52 and 1954–59), J. William Carter (1952–54), George Davis (1959–63), and H. A. J. Wedderburn (1963–95). It had paved the path for the new politics of the 1960s, for the spill-over from the American civil rights movement, for the birth of the National Black Coalition, the Black United Front, the Society for the Protection and Preservation of Black Culture in Nova Scotia, the Black Educators Association, and many other bodies—for the emergence of new strategies and new voices to tackle both old and new issues as a new world order was taking shape everywhere.

VIOLA DESMOND,
c.1950

At this time there was no national body to represent the emerging needs of the black population in Canada, a population that had been in Canada longer than any other non-European immigrant group. In 1969 a meeting was convened in Toronto and the National Black Coalition was established. Dr. Howard McCurdy of Windsor, Ontario, was elected its first president. After a most distinguished academic career, Dr. McCurdy went on to earn a prominent place in national politics as a member of parliament. His visits to Nova Scotia over many years were warmly received. He was a major contributor to the Canadian Black Studies Conference in Halifax in 1979.

DR. HOWARD McCURDY, FIRST PRESIDENT OF THE NATIONAL BLACK COALITION

The national body had a turbulent history of divisions and disunity, as remembered by Wilson Head in his memoir, *A Life on the Edge: Experiences in Black and White in North America*. He had been present at the founding meeting in 1969 and left a disappointed man. Head writes that by 1976 the national body was practically dead, but an attempt was made to re-establish it at a meeting in Halifax in 1978. He accepted the position of president, in spite of his reservations, because he wanted to see the organization survive. But, as he writes, the road ahead was strewn with obstacles and differences:

It only required two meetings of the executive committee before some of the old attitudes began to rise to the surface. Some attitudes were related to locality. For example, differences of opinion existed between the West Indian and the Canadian and American-born black populations, and even between blacks from the different islands of the West Indies.... By the end of the first year and the first Annual General Meeting of the new organization, the beginning of the self-destruction process was already evident.... It became very clear that the NBCC had embarked on a dangerous journey.

BURNLEY "ROCKY" JONES

Burnley "Rocky" Jones, long-time dynamic activist and outspoken scholar of the Nova Scotia scene, presented his case against the NBCC in an article entitled "Nova Scotia Blacks: A Quest for a Place in the Canadian Mosaic." He is critical of the leadership of West Indian immigrants which he describes as:

> *insensitive to and unaware of the problems faced by Blacks who do not live within the Montreal–Toronto axis.... Blacks in Nova Scotia, through their provincial organizations such as the Black Educators Association, the Black United Front, the Nova Scotia Human Rights Commission, the Dalhousie University Transition Year Program Students' Association and the NSAACP have attempted to make the federal government and the National Black Coalition aware of the misrepresentation of Black Canadians at the national level.... If the only solution to the plight of indigenous Blacks in Nova Scotia is to withdraw from our so-called national organization, so be it.... We are part of the founding peoples of Canada and as such we should have the opportunity to represent our own interests when those who purport to represent us, in fact, do not.*

By the mid-eighties the NBCC was in irreparable disarray, and shortly afterwards it ceased to exist. We turn, then, to the provincial organizations during the period of their foundation and early formative years.

DR. WILSON HEAD,
c.1980

The Black United Front (BUF) was born out of accidental events that occurred between November 1968 and August 1969, set in motion by an offshoot of the American civil rights movement. In November 1968 several Black Panther members led by Stokely Carmichael came to Halifax, in the words of a one-time executive director of the BUF, "at the invitation of some local activists. They began some organizing work and held a number of local meetings.... The activities of this group created considerable alarm both in the white and black communities of Nova Scotia, and the Panthers were persuaded to return to the US."

The author of the article cited, then known as Art Criss, now known as Hamid Rasheed, points out that this situation was picked up by existing black organizations, who agreed to hold a conference in Halifax, "to bring into the open the diversity in the black community between young and old, rural and urban, the indigenous population and the new arrivals from the West Indies. It also highlighted the lack of unity among blacks and the fact that there was no substantial agreement on problems, solutions, needs, objectives or strategies." These words mirror closely the words of Wilson Head and Burnley Jones in the context of the National Black Coalition.

Following a meeting of some four hundred members of the black community in the Halifax Regional Library in the last week of November 1968, an interim committee was struck under the chairmanship of Rev. William P. Oliver, comprising the following members, all drawn from the Halifax-Dartmouth metro area: Burnley Jones, Edith Gray, Ross Kinney, Keith Prevost, H. A. J. Wedderburn, Arnold Johnson, and Churchill Smith—all prominent members of the black community, associated in one way or other with the NSAACP or the AUBA, or with youth or civic politics. They had come together at a black family meeting—one of many that would be held in the province in the decades ahead. In Dr. Oliver's vision of the day, the new organization, not yet fleshed out, could well be an umbrella for the black community, one that would create unity through consensus. In an interview reported in the *Chronicle Herald* on January 2, 1969, Dr. Oliver likened the BUF to a catalytic body, "one of anti-violence, in favour of a new firmness, dignity, aggressiveness, even militance…wanting action in the immediate future."

Much was expected from the BUF. Because the organization had been formed so quickly, little groundwork had been laid. While it was firmly decided that the BUF was to be a black organization, there was less agreement on whether the organization ought to follow the path of radicalism. Was it to be a model of militant protest and a supporter of the militant programme of the Black Panther movement of the United States, or an organization committed to peaceful protest and quiet diplomacy in line with the philosophy and actions of earlier organizations in the province?

Three members of the interim committee—William Oliver, Gus Wedderburn, and Keith Prevost—presented the vision and programme of the vaunted "Black Consensus" to two representatives of the federal government: Gerald Pelletier, secretary of state, and Allan MacEachern, minister of manpower and immigration and the senior cabinet member from Nova Scotia. Their brief of January 20, 1969 was well formulated even if overstated. They had found a tool to repair centuries of hurtful damage:

Black people now for the first time in the history of the Nova Scotia Negro have collectively realized that their frustration emerges from the subtleties of racism and discrimination by the whites. They realize that they cannot fight the intangible thing called "discrimination" without some power to control it. It is hoped that the Black United Front would be the tool that would assist…to overcome the monotony of anxiety, frustration, poverty and depression caused by overt and insidious discrimination.

The interim committee spoke well and stated its goals well, making it harder for itself to achieve them as well: achievement of black consensus; attainment of economic, consumer, and political power; development of black leadership; research and documentation of problem areas; self-reliance—all with "cooperation and more Federal assistance."

The federal government came up with $100,000 for the first year for the appointment of an executive director and four field workers and for an extensive study of the black environment. The money came through in June 1969, almost at the same time as federal health minister John Munro visited the Preston area, bypassing county councillors of the area and making an ill-chosen remark about being "shocked at the deplorable conditions" that existed there. One of the members of the interim committee of the BUF, Councillor Arnold Johnson of North Preston, broke ranks when he said: "Mr. Munro was quoted in the local paper as saying the federal grant would help the BUF 'raise hell' by becoming a pressure group. The BUF didn't deny that they were a hell raising organization. It's my request to Dr. Oliver and his little hell raising group to stay the hell out of Preston." Once again, building consensus and unity of purpose in the black community proved to be difficult.

In the quarter-century of its existence (1969–95) the Black United Front was helmed by eight executive directors: Jules Oliver, Hamid Rasheed, George Borden (interim), Richard Joseph, Gerald Taylor, Yvonne Atwell, Winston Ruck, and Rev. Ogueri Ohanaka. Its fuller story needs to be told someday, even if it no longer exists. It is, after all, a part of the story of the African Nova Scotian past, the story of an experiment that faced many challenges and obstacles. When one looks at the BUF's board of directors, which included distinguished members of almost every black community in the province, one can't help but wonder why a more lasting legacy was not achieved.

GERALD CLARKE

Along with the BUF, the Black Educators Association also came into existence in 1969. As the name indicates, its mandate and its focus were clearly defined. The ongoing development of the black population depended largely on the education of its constituents. Thus there was an urgent role for educated blacks in the development of society in general and the black population in particular.

Segregated schools had been legislated by statute in 1884, reaffirmed in 1918, and not struck down until 1954. As late as 1936 there had been only three black university graduates in the history of Nova Scotia: Edwin Howard Borden (1869–1953), who was born in Truro and educated at Acadia University where he obtained a BA degree in 1892; James Robinson Johnston; and William Pearly Oliver. But there were other pioneers whose contribution reached far and wide, such as Madeline Symonds, who went to the Provincial Normal College in Truro in 1927 and graduated a year later as the first black woman teacher.

Because of the experience of segregation, black communities in Nova Scotia were always intimately involved with education. In the words of Alma F. Johnston, president of the Black Cultural Society, introducing the society's "Portrait of Retired Black Teachers: A Legacy of Nova Scotia's Black History" in 1991, "education has always been a vital part of the black community. The local communities controlled the schools. They selected teachers, maintained the school buildings, found living accommodations for the teachers and collected monies for the teachers' salaries.... " Johnston went on to point out that "the majority of the black teachers today were educated in segregated schools in Nova Scotia. The Diogenes Study Club, the Black Educators Association and the Black Professional Women's Group were formed by black teachers of segregated schools."

The segregated black settlements of the eighteenth and nineteenth centuries had their teachers, too, such as Colonel Blucke, Joseph Leonard, William Furmage, Catherine Abernathy, Thomas Brownspriggs, Dempsey Jordan, Isaac Limerick, and John Pleasant. Pleasant was also the first assistant clerk of the AUBA in 1854. The line of black teachers since then is a long and distinguished one, and this volume cannot pretend to provide a comprehensive account.

Synonymous with the place and prestige of black teachers in Nova Scotia society is the pioneering and outstanding work of the Black Educators Association formed in the period 1969–71. Predated by the work and thinking of the Diogenes Teachers' Study Club (in existence since the mid-fifties), led and supported by such early teachers as Delbert Hodges, H. A. J. Wedderburn, and Donna Lee Byard Sealey, a Negro Education Committee was set up in 1969 to investigate the quality of education for black students in Nova Scotia. Two years later, the Black Educators Association of Nova Scotia was formed out of the Negro Education Committee. The chairman during the foundation years of the Negro Education Committee/Black Educators Association was H. A. J. Wedderburn (1969–72). The leadership roles of five other individuals laid a solid foundation for the future of the BEA: Rev. Dr. Anna Hunter (1972–74), Bard Barton (1974–78 and 1983–87), Gerald Clarke (1978–80), Patricia Barton (1981–82), and Sheila Cole (1987–89). Of the members who served as presidents of the BEA, Gerald Clarke was appointed the first executive director. He had formidable qualifications: holder of a BSc, BEd, and an MEd, he began his teaching career in 1966 and went on to hold several senior administrative positions before he retired, including acting principal of Clayton Park Junior High School and principal of Fairview Junior High School.

BRAD BARTON. PROMINENT TEACHER, PRINCIPAL AND ADMINISTRATOR. AWARDED THE ORDER OF CANADA, IN 2000.

Of the scores of African Nova Scotian pioneering teachers, one who deserves special mention is Brad Barton, who rose to the top in many pursuits—never failing to encourage others, including students, parents, teachers, and politicians, to work in tandem in the interest of quality education. A graduate of the Nova Scotia Teachers College, he retired in 1997 after thirty-two years of teaching and several principalships, most notably at C. P. Allen High School in Bedford. He also served as sub-system supervisor and coordinator of race relations, cross-cultural understanding, and human rights. He was instrumental, earlier on, for broadening the scope of the BEA and ensuring, among other projects, that its first publication, *Beneath the Clouds of the Promised Land: The Survival of Nova Scotia Blacks*, became a reality. In 2000 Brad Barton was awarded the Order of Canada.

THE BLACK CULTURAL SOCIETY AND THE BLACK CULTURAL CENTRE

Rev. William Pearly Oliver, pastor of Cornwallis Street Baptist Church for many years, was always much concerned with the cultural progress of African Nova Scotians. In June 1949 he presented a paper on the subject to the Canadian Humanities Council's Maritime Regional Conference. The paper was published in the *Dalhousie Review* later that year. In hindsight, what he asked for was remarkably basic and can be seen as a commentary on the backwardness of Canadian and Nova Scotian society in 1949:

> *Let us begin by demanding that our school text books be examined and all that is predatory, objectionable, and without educational value be removed, in order that minority groups will not be offended.... Let colour and racial clauses be erased from scholarships.... Let hotels and restaurants cater to the public on the basis of individual behaviour, regardless of race. Let trade unions and employers give opportunity to all who meet the requirements of the particular trade or vocation.*

Almost a quarter of a century later, in 1972, with fair employment and accommodation legislation in place, and human rights legislation and institutions on the rise, Dr. Oliver formulated another proposal, this time for the establishment of a cultural education centre for the black residents of Nova Scotia. This time, he argued, such an institution should be sponsored by the Black United Front since it had province-wide representation in partnership with the Continuing Education Program of the Nova Scotia Department of Education— another body in which he had an influential role. His plan was two-fold: "providing programs utilizing materials, environment and content that will enable black people to develop a positive self-concept" and sharing these with the population at large "in order that the non-black population might learn to understand black history and culture." He saw the Black Cultural Education Centre as the logical third phase in a continuum where the first was the NSAACP and the second the BUF.

Dr. Oliver included charts to illustrate the level of need that would be met and the organizational structure that would produce the results.

Dr. Oliver was the early visionary, who in his lifetime straddled all three phases of the continuum and saw successes, modifications, and some failures along the way. What he could not have predicted was how his proposal would materialize. The provincial government, through the minister of recreation, Mr. Garnet Brown, hosted a luncheon meeting for invited members of the black community on October 26, 1974. The minister spoke on "Building Pride in Heritage" and urged those present to form a committee that would work towards the building of a Black Cultural Centre. Donald Oliver, a Halifax lawyer, was chosen as chairman and entrusted with the task of choosing nine other members from different parts of the province to constitute the first steering committee. He chose Rev. P. A. Best of Yarmouth, Geraldine Browning of Centreville, A. E. Criss of Dartmouth, Edith Cromwell of Bridgetown, Rev. D. E. Fairfax of Dartmouth, Neville Gibson of Sydney, Rev. W. P. Oliver of Lucasville, Ken Pinto of Halifax, and H. A. J. Wedderburn of Halifax. The secretary was Joan Browne of Halifax.

GUS WEDDERBURN, MAXINE BROOKS, SHARON ROSS, AND GERALD REGAN LOOKING AT A MODEL OF THE BLACK CULTURAL CENTRE

A comparison of this roster with that of the BUF's first board reveals many of the same members, but there was no indication at this stage that an umbrella organization was in the making, nor that the BUF would lead the way. The period between October 26, 1974, and September 17, 1983, when the Black Cultural Centre was officially opened, was a remarkably productive time. In less than a decade the African Nova Scotian community and its supporters in the private and public sectors managed to build a permanent institution to showcase black history and culture, an institution which has stood steadfast ever since. The Black Cultural Centre was built in Westphal, Nova Scotia, on grounds donated by the trustees of the Nova Scotia Home for Coloured Children. At present, Highway 7 divides the property of the NSHCC: on one side is the Black Cultural Centre; diagonally opposite stands the dwelling of the original NSHCC, and some hundred metres or so towards Dartmouth and Halifax there are its newer premises—all hallowed historical grounds for African Nova Scotians.

A provincial conference was held in May 1976 at which five future stages were proposed: that the guiding philosophy of the Black Cultural Centre should be the total portrayal of the achievements and activities of the black people of Nova Scotia; that the steering committee should make way for the formation and incorporation by statute of the Society for the Protection and Preservation of Black Culture in Nova Scotia—to be known in short as the Black Cultural Society; that the site for the centre should be on the grounds of the NSHCC, where a museum complex was to be constructed; that a hall of fame should be created; and that provisions should be made for an arts and crafts workshop, a library and learning centre, and facilities "for auxiliary functions such as dining and accommodation services."

This volume, in keeping with its coverage of the pioneering past, will not trace the later history of the society and centre beyond 1985. Within this framework it is possible to say that all of these goals have been met, except for the provision of dining and accommodation services.

The Black Cultural Society was incorporated on May 19, 1977, with the following executive members (designated in 1980 as the board of directors): Rev. J. C. Mack, Donald Oliver, Ken Pinto, Alice Croft, and Joan Browne, all from Halifax; Rev. D. E. Fairfax, and H. A. J. Wedderburn from Dartmouth; Rev. P. A. Best of Yarmouth; Winston Ruck and Neville Gibson of Sydney; Hazel Johnson of Annapolis County; Carrie Best of Pictou County; Jeannette Brown and Rev. W. Bryant of Colchester County; Pat Skinner and Lisle Clarke of Antigonish County; Rev. Donald Skeir, Carolyn Thomas, and Joyce Ross of Preston; Elsie Elms of Guysborough County; Rev. Anna Hunter and John Davidson of Cumberland County; and Ronald Gibson of Queens and Shelburne Counties.

OFFICIAL OPENING OF THE BLACK CULTURAL CENTRE, SEPTEMBER 17, 1983

Sharon Ross was appointed project coordinator and over a short period $1.2 million dollars was raised. The building was erected and officially opened at a most impressive and colourful outdoor ceremony on September 17, 1983, attended by civic, provincial, and federal dignitaries and members of the Nova Scotia community. The premier of the province, John M. Buchanan, was invested at the opening ceremony with the Ancient Order of the African Friendly Society, a society which had been founded by the first pastor of the Cornwallis Street Baptist Church in the 1830s. A day earlier, the federal minister for international trade, Gerald A. Regan, had been invested with the same order.

The Black Cultural Society was served over the years by a number of presidents who left their mark in many distinctive ways: Donald Oliver, Q.C. (1977–80), H. A. J. Wedderburn (1980–85), Geraldine Browning (1985–87), Ruth Johnson (1987–89), Alma Johnston (1989–91), Anne Simmons (1991–93), Betty Thomas (1993–94), and Brian Johnston (1994–). The centre's first executive director, who served for a short period, was Frank Boyd, followed by Wayne Adams on secondment from the civil service (1985–86), and Bridglal Pachai, who served first as programme director in 1985 and then as executive director from 1986 to 1989, when he was appointed to head the Nova Scotia Human Rights Commission. Maxine Brooks was appointed administrative secretary in 1980 and Henry Bishop was appointed curator in 1982 and later chief curator.

With limited resources, limited staff, and a broad and growing mandate, the Black Cultural Centre set out to implement the objectives set by its parent body, the Black Cultural Society. In its first few years, it published a number of books and anniversary lectures; carried out tours and speaking engagements; collected, labelled, and displayed artifacts; conducted workshops; and hosted a weekly television programme on the African Nova Scotian experience. The centre also had its difficult financial days, during which the AUBA intervened to suggest a merger with the BUF. The full story of this interlude is outside the scope of this volume, but suffice it to say the merger never came through. Since then, the Black Cultural Society and the Black Cultural Centre, with prudent planning and management, have overcome their difficulties, settled their mortgage commitments, held an emotional mortgage-burning ceremony at the centre, and continued on their forward journey.

Chapter 7

Glimpses of Military and Sports Personalities

MEMBERS OF THE NO. 2 CONSTRUCTION BATTALION, C.1916

Blacks in Canada have, ever since their arrival and settlement, readily and generously volunteered their military service in defence of liberty and freedom. As James Walker, foremost pioneer, researcher, and author in this field, has stated in a comprehensive paper, "On the Record: The Testimony of Canada's Black Pioneers, 1783–1865," "Throughout the 1840s and 50s blacks remained 'on guard' for Canada in the provincial militias of Ontario, New Brunswick and Nova Scotia, and in both Hamilton, Ontario and Victoria, Vancouver Island, blacks created their own volunteer rifle corps."

There were many reasons for this readiness and willingness to render service, not least of which were the social and economic environment, as well as the opportunities for gainful employment, personal dignity, and development. Four pioneering naval personalities from Nova Scotia illustrate these points: William Hall, John Perry, Joseph B. Noil, and Benjamin Jackson.

The place of William Hall is quite remarkable. His place in history is that of the first Canadian seaman, the first Nova Scotian, and the first person of African descent to be awarded the Victoria Cross—the British Empire's highest award for bravery. Born of Black refugee parents at Horton in the Annapolis Valley on either April 25, 1828, or April 26, 1829, (both dates are given in the historical lore and baptismal certificate), he grew up in Hantsport, centre of the wooden shipbuilding industry, where both father and son worked for the Halifax ship-owner Samuel Cunard. At age fifteen William Hall went on a trading vessel to the United States and at age eighteen he joined the United States Navy. A year later, at the age of nineteen, he took part in the Mexican War of 1848. In 1852 he enlisted in the Royal Navy, served on various battleships, took part in the Crimean War (1855–56), and soon after found himself a member of the crew of *HMS Shannon* on naval exercise while stationed in Hong Kong. From leading gunner, he was promoted to captain of the foretop.

In August 1857 the *Shannon* responded to the call from the British government for help in suppressing a rebellion that had broken out in India against the rule of the British East India Company— the so-called Indian Mutiny or Indian Rebellion. It was in the Relief of Lucknow, on November 16, 1857, that William Hall's bravery commended him, when the two-cannon gun crew of the *Shannon* lost twelve men, and William Hall remained alone to load, fire, and reload the twenty-four-pounder cannon, with bullets directed at him from a fortress. Hall was a strong man and was able to keep up a steady fire while dragging the cannon backward and forward to load and reload. At last the wall was breached and the soldiers entered.

WILLIAM NEILSON HALL

For his gallantry, William Hall received the Victoria Cross on February 15, 1859, joining three others for outstanding bravery on that battlefield and becoming the third Canadian to be awarded the Victoria Cross. He retired from the Royal Navy in 1876 with the rank of first class petty officer, returned to the Annapolis Valley, and settled on his farm on the Bluff Road, Avonport, where he died in 1904. In addition to the Victoria Cross, Hall had also received other distinguished military honours: the Crimean War Medal with bars for Inkerman and Sebastopol, the Turkish Medal for service in the Crimea, and the Indian

Mutiny Medal with bars for the Battle of Lucknow and the Relief of Lucknow.

At the time William Hall was sailing the seas, another sailor from Annapolis Royal, John Perry, nicknamed "The Black Sailor," followed his father's footsteps and served in a British warship (1845–50). Unlike Hall, Perry ran afoul of the law, was convicted, and was sent off to the convict settlement of Australia, where his huge muscular frame won him the heavyweight boxing crown of Australia on December 10, 1849. Perry did not return to Annapolis Royal.

After Hall and Perry came another black Nova Scotian seaman, Joseph B. Noil, born in 1841. Noil enlisted in the US Navy in 1871. While serving in the United States steamer *Powhatan* in 1872, Joseph Noil rescued a fellow crewman who had fallen overboard in the raging ocean waters. For his act of valour, Joseph B. Noil was awarded the Medal of Honour—the highest award then bestowed upon a serviceman in the United States for gallantry.

Thus, as a forerunner to the outstanding military contribution of men and women of African Nova Scotian descent in the twentieth century, we have the sterling examples of three black seamen—all born in the Annapolis Valley—serving in British and American warships and earning the highest award in their fields either during service or after service.

THE FUNERAL PROCESSION OF WILLIAM HALL, VC, 1904

RELATIVES OF WILLIAM HALL, VC, IN FRONT OF HIS MEMORIAL CAIRN, 1947

A fourth seaman whose life spans both centuries (1835–1915) is Benjamin Jackson, born in Lockhartville, Kings County, also in the Annapolis Valley, not far from the birthplace of William Hall. A brief account of Benjamin Jackson appears in an article by Don Duncanson published in *The Nova Scotia Genealogist*. Jackson enlisted in the US Navy during the American Civil War for a three-year period (1864–67), but was honourably discharged in June 1865 after being wounded on active service. He died on September 4, 1915, and was buried in an unmarked graveyard at Stoney Hill, Lockhartville, midway between Hantsport and Grand Pré. This was where William Hall was buried when he died in 1904, before his remains were reinterred in 1945 on the grounds of the Hantsport Baptist Church. But Benjamin Jackson is no longer a little-known name. His name has replaced the former Lockhartville Road which crosses Highway 101 west of Hantsport. The conspicuous road sign bearing his name has become familiar to those who travel to and from Nova Scotia's famous Annapolis Valley.

A year before Benjamin Jackson died, World War I broke out in Europe and in quick and devastating stages spread directly or indirectly to affect the whole world. Labelled "the war to end all wars," it never lived up to its lofty label, but it succeeded in changing the course of world history forever. Black Canadians, like their predecessors mentioned in these pages, were willing to rally to the call to defend liberty and human dignity, but they faced numerous obstacles in that age when imperialism and colonialism loomed large in the British Empire. Black men who tried to enlist were routinely turned away by white recruiting officers. After the black leaders managed to make a national issue of this rejection, the military finally decided to create an all-black unit in April 1916. The unit that resulted was the No. 2 Construction Battalion, the only segregated black battalion in the history of the Canadian military. Some blacks also managed to join other battalions, such as the 106th Battalion (Nova Scotia Rifles). The story of these veterans has been told over the years in different contexts, with varying emphases. Robin W. Winks told the story first, in broad but well-researched strokes, in his book *The Blacks in Canada: A History* (1971). A more intimate and individual effort followed in Calvin W. Ruck's book *Canada's Black Battalion: No. 2. Construction 1916–1920* (1986), later reissued as *The Black Battalion, 1916–1920: Canada's Best Kept Military Secret.* The subtitle of this second edition points to the shameful lack of recognition accorded to these black veterans. This recognition finally came in July 1993, when the Historic Sites and Monuments Board of Canada and the Black Cultural Society of Nova Scotia, in cooperation with the town of Pictou, unveiled a memorial plaque on the Pictou Market Wharf, where the headquarters of No. 2 Construction Battalion, Canadian Expeditionary Force, was first set up on July 5, 1916.

Le Camp des Noirs - La Prison

No. 2 Construction Battalion in Jura, France

On November 12, 1982, the Black Cultural Society hosted a recognition banquet for black veterans of World War I. The images in this book of those black patriots who served in this and other battalions remind us of an era when their patriotism was poorly received because of skin colour, but gloriously fulfilled on the battlefields of Europe. The last of the surviving Nova Scotia black veterans of World War I was Deacon Sydney Morgan Jones of Truro, Nova Scotia, who died in Halifax on December 20, 1993. He was one of sixteen blacks to enlist in the 106th Battalion. Private Sydney Jones was wounded at Passchendale, Belgium. A charter member of the NSAACP, Sydney Jones served for forty-two years as deacon of the Cornwallis Street Baptist Church.

THE REUNION OF WORLD WAR I VETERANS AT THE BLACK CULTURAL CENTRE, 1982

BACK ROW: SEYMOUR TYLER, SYDNEY JONES, ISAAC PHILLS, JOHN PANNILL FRONT ROW: WILLIAM CARTER, JOHN HAMILTON, MR. SMITH, FRED WILSON

Another distinguished World War I veteran was an uncle of Sydney Jones, Private Jeremiah Jones, also from Truro, who died in 1951. Half a century later he was honoured for his contribution and bravery, when the Truro branch of the Royal Canadian Legion erected a memorial stone at the Robie Street cemetery in Truro. Jones had been recommended for a Distinguished Conduct Medal for bravery in August 1917 at Vimy Ridge as a member of the 106th Battalion. He never got the medal, though he earned the respect of his peers.

Black war veterans of World War I paved the way for the many who followed in later times and later wars, men such as Roy Wellington States from New Glasgow. States was only twenty when World War II broke out in 1939. He turned up quickly for enlistment and equally swiftly was sent home with the admonition that blacks had no place in a "white man's war." The refrain of an earlier time was sounded over and over throughout the land, but this time the new generation persisted. Wellington States was finally enlisted in 1940 and served in the Canadian Armed Forces for twenty-five years.

Alan Bundy of Dartmouth joined the Royal Canadian Air Force in 1943, becoming the first black Nova Scotian to be recruited for aircrew training. He went on forty-two missions overseas. At the time of his discharge in 1946, he held the rank of flying officer. Calvin Ruck, who interviewed Bundy in 1984, noted in *The Black Battalion* that Bundy was first rejected on racial grounds in 1939. A change of commanding officers in Halifax in 1943 led to his acceptance.

George Borden from New Glasgow joined the RCAF in 1953, rising to the rank of lieutenant in 1967 and captain in 1970. After a thirty-two-year career with the air force, Captain Borden retired on December 17, 1985. He was the youngest of three brothers who served in the Canadian Armed Forces, the others being Wilfred and Curtis. An avid poet, historian, and writer on the subject of blacks in the military, George Borden used his military experience to continue to serve Nova Scotian society after his retirement.

He recalls his knowledge of the military in the following words:

Between 1939–45 many Blacks lined the ranks of Canada's contribution to defeat Hitler. Most healthy black males served in the European theatre and at sea, a number of whom made the ultimate sacrifice…. After a brief lull in military recruitment between 1945–48, the call went out for a 'peace-time force.'… They have served their country well in war-time Korea and peace-time Egypt, Cyprus, Europe and many other uneasy parts of the…world.

The many black veterans Borden alludes to are deserving of more attention in a larger volume yet to be written. The few selected in these pages are but a small part of the big picture. Oscar Seale of Sydney enlisted in 1941; after the war he promoted athletics and baseball. Thomas Miller enlisted in 1943, became an instructor who was trained at Aldershot, the famous military base in England, and at war's end joined the Whitney Pier Air Cadets, which he served for fourteen years. In his illustrious post-war life, Thomas Miller became the first black alderman in eastern Canada when he was elected to the Sydney City Council—a position he held for seventeen years. A few other pioneers must be mentioned here: Cyril Albert Clayton, who enlisted in 1958 and rose to the rank of chief warrant officer and regimental sergeant major before retiring in 1996 after thirty-eight years of distinguished service; Chief Warrant Officers John Madison and Raymond Lawrence; and Warrant Officers John Bowden and Angus Paris.

When a fuller account of the black contribution to Canada's military appears, it will have to recognize the talents and educational attainments of African Nova Scotians who enlisted. Here we give the examples of Traffic Control Officer Philip Waring Oliver of the RCAF and Major Marguerite (Peggy) Downes, both of whom went on to occupy positions that were not previously open to blacks in the military. Both served these positions well and in their time became pioneers who broke barriers.

Philip Oliver, son of Rev. William P. Oliver and Dr. Pearleen Oliver, already mentioned in earlier sections, graduated from Queen Elizabeth High School in Halifax, winning the Jack Cromwell Award for the male student showing the highest qualities of manhood and character. He proceeded to Acadia University, where he obtained the degrees of bachelor of science, master of science, and bachelor of education. He went on to be the principal of the Chibougamau Protestant School in Trois-Rivières, Quebec. He died on June 28, 1981.

Marguerite Downes was born in Dartmouth, Nova Scotia. Her brother, Leo Brown, served in World War II. In 1956 Downes moved to Toronto, wrote and passed the Ontario Civil Service Examination with a perfect mark, studied nursing, and enlisted in the army in 1957, rising to the rank of deputy commanding officer of the Canadian Forces Communications Reserve Unit. Major Downes was the first commissioned and highest ranking African Canadian woman in the Canadian military up to the time of her retirement in 1988, after thirty-two years of meritorious service.

ORVAL BROWNING RECEIVING A MODEL OF THE AURORA, 1977

Orval Browning, presently living in Centreville in the Annapolis Valley, has a number of pieces of military history attached to his military career: firstly, nineteen years of service in the Royal Canadian Navy starting December 30, 1949; secondly, eleven years in the air force from 1968 to 1979; thirdly, fourteen years in the Reserve Air Cadets Glider Operations, giving him some forty-four years in both the regular and reserve units—a length of service not easily matched. With three bars to his Canadian Forces Decoration, Orval Browning surely qualifies to be the longest serving black member of the Canadian air force's regular and reserve units. Another piece of Warrant Officer Browning's military history is that he named the Aurora aircraft prior to going to Egypt in the fall of 1975, for which he received a certificate and a model of the Aurora from Defence Minister Barney Danson at CFB Greenwood in January 1977.

LIEUTENANT-COLONEL ROBERT MAXWELL

Until his retirement, the highest ranking black officer in the Canadian Armed Forces was Lieutenant-Colonel Robert Maxwell, who enlisted in the Canadian Air Force in 1956 and retired in 1993, holding the position of Canadian Forces fire marshal. A graduate of Saint Mary's University in Halifax and the Canadian Forces Staff School in Toronto, Robert Maxwell is a fitting personality with whom to end this section on the pioneering contribution of African Nova Scotians to military history.

As an institution, the military was a mirror of society. As in the wider society, the men and women listed in this section faced racial discrimination. They struggled at first to be enlisted, and were told to go home, until a segregated construction battalion was started in 1916. Some white commanders kept on objecting, using the same racial stereotypes prevalent outside the military. In 2004, Retired Flight Lieutenant Sam Estwick, at age eighty-nine, spoke of his experiences with this kind of discrimination. Born in Barbados, he came to Glace Bay, Cape Breton, before school age. With good grades he came to Halifax to enlist in 1940, but was told he could not enlist as a pilot because he was black. He went to Clinton, Ontario, joined and trained, and proceeded to serve in India, North Africa, Europe, and South Africa. His problems in society and in the pursuit of his career were surely not isolated.

The development of a segregated society due to the existence of the colour line in Nova Scotia—and all over Canada—contributed to the existence of separate institutions and activities. We have already noted that separate churches and schools existed for black residents. Separate sporting activities followed when black communities formed their own baseball and hockey teams, leading to the formation of associations and the holding of championships. All-black hockey teams existed as early as 1895, and the Colored Hockey League of the Maritimes was formed by 1900, with headquarters in Halifax. At the time of its formation, it received help and advice from two young members of the community whose contributions to the advancement of black youth have already been discussed in some detail: James R. Johnston and J. A. R. Kinney. The league existed till the 1920s. It had two main teams in Halifax and one in Dartmouth: the Halifax Eurekas, the Halifax Stanley, and the Dartmouth Jubilees.

James A. R. Kinney, at age nineteen, took over as chief organizer of the Colored Hockey League. Kinney, young, educated, diplomatic, and visionary, never gave up a challenge in his illustrious career in education, business, church, and social service. At that stage in his life he was promoting black sports as a means of realizing black upliftment. Without any regular arenas to play in, and no newspaper coverage for black hockey, it was relegated to frozen ponds surrounding Africville: Tibby's Pond and Southwestern Field. In later years the Colored Hockey League grew and matured: the Eureka team emerged as the league's flagship; the Africville Sea-Sides emerged as a strong team; players like Frank L. Symonds and John Brown Jr. became well-known. George and Darril Fosty in their book about the league, *Black Ice*, list more: Augustus and George Adams, Stanley Johnson, and John Mansfield. Soon an all-white Halifax Senior League was formed and black teams, which had managed to get into proper arenas, found themselves last on the list for ice time.

AFRICVILLE BROWN BOMBERS The earliest years of black hockey had made their mark in spite of considerable difficulties. By the 1930s there were four black hockey teams in Halifax: the West End Rangers, Cherrybrook, Halifax Hawks, and Africville Brown Bombers. In addition, the Halifax Colored Citizen, Improvement League, mentioned in Chapter 6, contributed significantly to sports and recreation after 1932, organizing summer camps for needy children and sponsoring a hockey team. The founder and president of the improvement league, Beresford Augustus Husbands, had for long championed the idea of building a cultural and educational youth centre. Sadly, he died a year before this was realized when the George Dixon Community Recreation Centre opened in the North End of Halifax on August 11, 1969.

GEORGE DIXON

The name of George Dixon takes us to boxing, another sport in which pioneering African Nova Scotians excelled in the local, regional, national, and international arenas. George Dixon led the way. Born in Africville on July 29, 1870, this young man of slight build, 5 feet 3 inches tall, weighing a little over one hundred pounds, rose rapidly. He eventually held two world titles, but sadly for the sport and for his community, he died in 1909 at the age of thirty-nine. As a teenager he worked out at a modest gymnasium in Creighton Street, Halifax, while he worked in a photographer's studio nearby, marvelling at the boxers who dropped in to have their pictures taken. He had his first professional fight in Halifax and moved soon after to Boston, where, at twenty, he won the world bantamweight title, and a year later the world featherweight crown. The "Little Chocolate"— as he was nicknamed—had put Africville on the map. It wasn't easy, nor were the times propitious, as Charles Saunders emphasizes in *Sweat and Soul: The Saga of Black Boxers from the Halifax Forum to Caesar's Palace:*

The magnitude of George Dixon's feat can best be appreciated within the context of its time. In 1890, race relations around the world had entered a period some historians call "The Nadir," the lowest point. Blacks were disenfranchised and terrorized in the U.S. South, swept under the rug in the U.S. North and excluded from immigration to Canada. Only five years before, the European powers had partitioned the entire continent of Africa. And now a black man was champion of a world in which those who questioned white supremacy were either silenced or ignored.

SAM LANGFORD

The other African Nova Scotian boxer of international fame was Sam Langford, a contemporary of George Dixon. He was born in the segregated black settlement of Weymouth Falls, in western Nova Scotia. Dixon's and Langford's paths were almost parallel: the first, fourteen years older, with two world crowns, died young; the second, with some 642 bouts under his belt, lost his eyesight as the wear and tear from these fights took its toll. Both fought out of Boston; both were nicknamed with racial undertones: one the "Little Chocolate," the other the "Boston Tar Baby." The former travelled the world with his crowns safely on; the latter travelled the world as the uncrowned heavyweight champion of the world—unable to get a title fight to give him a chance, so feared was he by his peers. In recognition of their courage to take on the unequal barriers of their time, both were inducted into the World Boxing Hall of Fame. And for the legacy of black boxing pioneers in Nova Scotia, both have community centres named after them: the George Dixon Community Centre in Halifax and the Sam Langford Community Centre in Weymouth Falls. Both Dixon and Langford died outside Canada: Dixon in New York City (1909) and Langford in Cambridge, Massachusetts (1956).

Nova Scotia has produced other remarkable black boxers who earned fame in the Maritimes and nationally. On October 1, 1988, the Black Cultural Centre for Nova Scotia held the first Nova Scotia Black Boxers' Reunion and Remembrance Dinner at the Sheraton Hotel in Halifax. The chair of the organizing committee, Delmore "Buddy" Daye, himself a former Canadian lightweight and Maritime featherweight champion, was assisted by four other members: Ricky Anderson, former Canadian welterweight champion; Murray Langford, boxing promoter and trainer; and the two authors of this volume. It was a tremendous reunion and remembrance night, graced by Premier John Buchanan, former world heavyweight champion Jersey Joe Walcott, and a whole host of notable boxers. The list of invitees included Keith Paris, Dexter Connors, Leroy Lawrence, Jesse Elroy Mitchell, Leroy Jones, Cecil Gray, Kevin Downey, Joe Pile, Arnold Sparks, Bryan Gibson, Ozzie Farral, Al MacLean, Sherry Lawrence, Billy Downey, and Lawrence States. Former and current greats were also celebrated: George Dixon, Sam Langford, "Buddy" Daye, Ricky Anderson, the Canadian and Commonwealth welterweight champion Clyde Gray, and Dave Downey, an all-round athlete who won the Canadian Middleweight Championship in 1967. His son, Raymond Downey, was, at the time of the reunion, the Canadian Amateur Light Middleweight champion and was preparing to represent his country at the Seoul Olympics.

DELMORE "BUDDY" DAYE

In an interview prior to the event, chairman "Buddy" Daye presented some touching insights into the travails of a black boxer's life in pioneering times:

Back then, no matter how good you were, they didn't want a black fighter to head-line a card.... All of them sacrificed a lot and they were real trailblazers. They paved the way for the fighters of today.

In 2003 Ricky Anderson, one of the honorees mentioned above and a member of the committee that organized the Nova Scotia Black Boxers' Reunion and Remembrance Night, wrote a book entitled *Win In The Arena of Life: Living a Life You Love Is Worth Fighting For.* It, of course, tells more than the stories about winning the Canadian Welterweight Championship, important as that was. It speaks to the ethos of discipline, faith, courage, and education—all of which were cornerstones of the successes of the boxing pioneers. Ricky Anderson acquired an education that enabled him to use his fame and talents to serve himself and his society outside the boxing arena. Few, if any, before him had had that opportunity. As Delmore "Buddy" Daye said years later: "I never liked to fight. I didn't feel good when I lost and I didn't feel good when I won. I was just trying to make a living, provide for my family."

In the process, Daye and the other sports pioneers provided a source of inspiration and a legacy that lives on in black Nova Scotia.

Chapter 8

Pioneers in the Arts

THE PLANTATION FOUR, A NEW GLASGOW GOSPEL GROUP, C.1920S

The combined influence and impact on the black community, from pioneering days to the present, of the pulpit, the piano, and the pen can be seen throughout every generation. Pastors and teachers were talented musicians; every home could boast of some instrument or other whose sounds and rhythm, verse and verve, went beyond entertainment, beyond spirituality, into the never-faltering search for a better place in society. In the story of pioneers, many families and individuals loom large. The family of William Andrew White is a case in point. Rev. Dr. White's place in church and military history is well known. But there were other sides to his life: scholar, athlete, teacher, singer, and radio producer. With the support of the Cornwallis Street Baptist Choir, broadcast over CHNS radio, his messages mixed with uplifting music reached wide audiences in Canada and the United States.

PORTIA WHITE

Under the influence of two musically talented parents, the White family children carried the pioneering torch forward. Portia White (1911–68) blazed a trail unsurpassed in the musical and artistic history of African Nova Scotians. From being a member of her father's church choir at age six, Portia rose in the musical world with such amazing rapidity that commentators could say in hindsight that this needed to be done for life was short. For a brief time, economic necessity saw a combination of university study, school teaching, and music lessons. She taught school in Africville, Lucasville, and in Westphal at the Home for Colored Children; studied for a teaching certificate at Dalhousie University; studied business at the Halifax County Academy; and studied music at the Halifax Conservatory of Music. When she made her Town Hall debut in New York City, the *New York Herald Tribune* reported as follows on March 14, 1944:

> *Portia White, contralto, showed the public…that she not only has a magnificent vocal instrument but that she also has sufficient musicianship and intelligence to do what she wishes with it. Scattered throughout her varied program were passages of superb singing, done in strong, straightforward fashion and with a purity of tonal quality the like of which one encounters all too seldom.*

Other newspaper reports on the same day wrote of "an exceptional voice...we shall hear a great deal more from her." Indeed, both Europe and North America heard this magical voice many times, as Portia White went on to a brilliant career. After touring the world and attaining considerable fame, she eventually settled in Toronto, where she taught voice lessons. In 1964 she performed for Queen Elizabeth II at the opening of the Confederation Centre of the Arts in Charlottetown. This was to be one of her last major performances before her death in 1968. In that year, the Nova Scotia Talent Trust created the Portia White Memorial Award in honour of the first recipient of the Nova Scotia Talent Trust Award, twenty-five years earlier in 1943. It was this award that had enabled Portia White to continue with her music studies.

DR. LORNE WHITE

Her youngest sister, Yvonne White, also studied voice for several years at the Maritime Conservatory of Music, the successor of the Halifax Conservatory. She has performed widely in Canada and the United States in drama and musical theatre, as well as solo renditions of sacred music, spirituals in particular. Both Yvonne and brother Lorne White were chosen to perform in the Canadian premiere of Gershwin's "Porgy and Bess" at the 1988 Olympics in Calgary. Dr. Lorne White, a retired school vice-principal and graduate of Acadia and Dalhousie universities has carried forward the family artistic talents and education, performing on CBC radio and television. All the while, true to family tradition, Dr. Lorne White has continued to serve many public causes in many positions.

In the same years when Rev. William Andrew White was overseas (1916–17), Blanche (Mrs. Morris V.) Davis was the first and only black person to graduate in piano and voice from the Halifax Ladies College and Conservatory of Music, which was one institution at that time. Mrs. Davis later returned to the Halifax Conservatory of Music to continue with her studies in piano. A member of the Criterion Club in Halifax, Blanche Davis was the mother of lawyer George Davis, one of the pioneering black lawyers.

One of Nova Scotia's most distinguished classical vocalists is Rev. Donald Edward Fairfax, whose contributions as a pastor are profiled in Chapter 3. He studied under Dr. Ernest DeVinci in the voice department of the Halifax Conservatory, and graduated in 1953. He gave his first recital at the Cornwallis Street Baptist Church. As a concert artist, Rev. Fairfax's rich baritone voice was highly acclaimed. He won many trophies and awards in his long music career, during which he also taught in the voice department of his alma mater.

Many other parts of the province have had their artistic contributors, too, such as Lucky Campbell, singer, songwriter, and musician from Lincolnville, who performed in different parts of Canada and the United States. Over the years, Campbell worked with the Mulgrave Road Theatre Group and Theatre Antigonish.

THE GOSPEL HEIRS, C.1990

The Gospel Heirs—a group of 7 family members from North Preston—organized themselves as a musical group in 1979. This group specialized in gospel-blues and performed in near and distant places, such as the Atlantic Gospel Music Convention, the African Festival in Quebec City, and Expo '86. Though no longer in existence as a group, their fame, name, and music live on. Their album *In the Light Today* was launched in 1995.

There are others, not quite old enough to be called "pioneers," but important in their time for their outstanding contribution and exemplary talents. Among them, Four the Moment performed in numerous venues including Expo '86. Suzanne Herbert, vocalist and actor from Glace Bay, had the same exposure at Expo '86 and also appeared on the CBC television series *New Faces*. She appeared in many theatre performances, as well as at the Charlottetown Festival. Charles "Bucky" Adams of Halifax, genial and loud, pioneered an uncommon path as a saxophonist starting in his teenage years in the early 1950s. In 1966 he played with the legendary Louis Armstrong and followed this up with the release of his album *"Bucky" Adams and the Basin Street Trio*. With over fifty years in the music industry, "Bucky" Adams has inspired budding musicians, taken music to the smaller communities, and promoted black pride, sense of community, and love of music.

WALTER BORDEN

The brothers George and Walter Borden, originally from New Glasgow, have made a distinctive contribution to the arts: George Borden in military history, poetry, and song writing; Walter Borden as an actor in radio dramas and stage and television plays. George Borden's earlier books on cultural poetry were *Canadian Odyssey* and *Footprints, Images and Reflections*. Walter Borden's earlier superb performances include *Tartuffe*, *Tightrope Time*, *God's Trombones*, and *Shine Boy*—the last-named written and directed by George Boyd, journalist and playwright. George Boyd was born and raised in Halifax and was the first African Nova Scotian news anchor on CBC Newsworld. His two works for screen are *Consecrated Ground* and *Dead Reckonining: The Lanier Phillips Story*. Besides *Shine Boy*, his other stage play—in which Walter Borden also acted—was *Gideon's Blues*.

In an interview shortly after the 1988 premiere of *Shine Boy*, a musical biography of George Dixon, George Boyd said:

> *I am black and I am a writer in Halifax, but I hope I have something to say that goes beyond those two facts. I hope Canadian theatre is ready for a black playwright. But I see myself, first as a playwright, period.*

George Boyd's words speak volumes for the many—some mentioned in these pages—whose earliest steps were taken in the family and the black community, but whose energies and aspirations always had as their goal a place and an acceptance in the Canadian community at large.

GEORGE ELLIOTT CLARKE

The accomplishments of Dr. George Elliott Clarke exemplify this point. Young in years, this African Nova Scotian—who champions the use of the word he coined, "Africadian"—has already blazed a pioneering trail as professor, poet, author, and playwright. His *Whylah Falls* was staged in Halifax and was adapted for radio and aired on CBC; *Beatrice Chancy* was performed on stage and broadcast on CBC TV. Among many other works, he wrote the screenplay for the film *One Heart Broken into Song*. A multi-faceted artist, he has won numerous awards, including the Portia White Award for Artistic Achievement and the Governor General's Award for English Poetry. In 2005 he received the prestigious Pierre Elliot Trudeau Award for outstanding contribution to scholarship.

Sylvia Hamilton—whose mother Dr. Marie Hamilton was herself a pioneer in church, teaching, and community service—co-directed her first film, *Black Mother, Black Daughter*, in 1987; it was screened by the National Film Board in 1989. Besides profiling her mother, Sylvia Hamilton's film includes others also mentioned in the present study, such as Daurene Lewis, Pearleen Oliver, Edith Clayton, and Four the Moment. A former journalist, researcher, writer, and more recently a distinguished filmmaker, Dr. Sylvia Hamilton's other films include *Speak It: From the Heart of Black Nova Scotia*, *Against the Tides*, *No More Secrets*, and *Portia White: Think on Me*. Sylvia Hamilton has also formed her film company, Maroon Films, which is located in Grand Pré, Nova Scotia.

Maxime Tynes, born and raised in Dartmouth, a school teacher by profession, has a prominent place in African Nova Scotia as a gifted poet. Author of two books of poetry, *Borrowed Beauty* and *Woman Talking Women*, Maxime Tynes won the People's Poet Award in 1988. She also worked for some time as a freelance broadcaster with CBC Radio. As the back cover of her *Borrowed Beauty* aptly puts it, Maxime Tynes "stands centre-stage as a vigorous Canadian poet with something very special to say"—words close to the vision of fellow writer George Boyd, quoted above.

EDITH CLAYTON

In the creative arts, the head, heart, and hands combine to produce exquisite products—like the legendary basket-weaving of a Canadian and Nova Scotian icon, Edith Clayton, who died on October 8, 1989, at a church service in her longtime church, East Preston United Baptist Church. In Joleen Gordon's *Edith Clayton's Market Basket: A Heritage of Splitwood Basketry in Nova Scotia*, we learn that Edith Clayton was born Edith Drummond on September 6, 1920. She was born into a basket-weaving family and learned the art from watching her mother. Her parents made a living by taking their baskets and vegetable produce weekly to the Halifax Market. Edith Clayton's maternal grandmother, born Mary Jackson in 1862, was also a basket-weaver, as was her maternal great-grandmother. Edith Clayton passed on the tradition of red maple basketry to her children, her neighbours, and her students; she also appeared at numerous craft events all over Nova Scotia, in Ottawa, at Expo '86 in Vancouver, and at the Harbour Front in Toronto. The recipient of numerous awards and honorary memberships, Edith Clayton, ever smiling, never failing to help and teach, left a permanent legacy for the craft guilds of Canada. From Cherrybrook to East Preston, from very humble beginnings and through hard work day in and day out, Edith Clayton wove split-wood baskets into more than market products, transforming them into symbols of pride and quality.

Chapter 9

Pioneers in Business, Labour, Politics, and Volunteerism

THE MARKETPLACE, HALIFAX, 19TH CENTURY

In 1964 Rev. William P. Oliver, then a regional representative in the adult education division of the Nova Scotia Department of Education, undertook a project to visit forty-seven black communities with an approximate total population of 14,000. In his report he made no mention of any business ventures on a high scale anywhere. He also made no reference to basket-weaving, which, as we have noted, existed since the 1830s. What he did note was some small measure of subsistence activity: self-employed gardeners, hog farmers, and wood vendors in Cherrybrook; the same in East Preston, where he noted that the soil was good but capital and know-how were lacking; he noted a thriving construction industry, bolstered by specialized business in rock masonry, concrete walks, and floors in the Lucasville Road area; farming and lumbering on Guysborough Road (near the present Halifax airport); and in the Hammonds Plains area, lumbering, coopers, and shops that sold barrels to orchardists and potato growers—though Oliver noted that demand was declining for the goods sold in these shops. The survey, although important in other areas, omitted to look at what may suitably be described as individual business initiatives, of which there were many examples, some of which now follow.

Jack and Viola Desmond opened a barber shop on Gottingen Street in 1932 and ran it till 1952. They called their shop Viola's Hairdressing and Jack's Barber Shop. Jack prided himself, with justification, on being the only registered black barber in Nova Scotia. He was joined later by Sydney Jones, already mentioned in Chapter 7, upon Jones's return from World War I. George Roache was an early restauranteur, with a restaurant at Gerrish and Gottingen streets in Halifax, mentioned in many accounts as a most popular dining place, where his wife Josephine prepared the finest pies in town.

The small grocery store was a popular initiative throughout the province, and it provided opportunities when few others were available. Florence Diggs is an excellent example. She kept a grocery store for forty-three years in East Preston. It was, by popular accounts, more than a business: it was a virtual community gathering place, as well as a postal outlet.

The Cape Breton example of Alexander and Daisy Parris is an immigrant success story: Alexander Parris came from Barbados to work in the Sydney Steel plant, where he worked for five years and then opened a shoe repair shop on Tupper Street. This enterprising couple kept moving up through long hours of work, soon buying their own house, running a candy and grocery store, and getting into the real estate business. Alexander Parris was also a talented musician who gave music lessons. He died in 1945. Daisy Parris was interviewed by the Black Cultural Centre in 1986, then eighty-nine years old, and died three years later.

In his time, Beresford Augustus Husbands, also born in Barbados, and mentioned in Chapter 6 of this book, was a successful businessman of many initiatives in Halifax: real estate, import-export, and fruit and vegetable sales—a merchant man and public figure much respected.

The story of Viola Davis Desmond, wife and business partner of Jack Desmond, is regrettably not well known for her strong business initiative as an entrepreneur in her own right. She was the founder and proprietor of Essential Grooming Ltd. and also the Desmond Studio of Beauty Culture, both established in the 1940s. Consider this letter written by Viola Desmond to the Ladies Auxiliary and Helping Hand Societies of the AUBA churches: "This is an honest effort to operate self-supporting shops; to train and employ as many young people as possible within our race. The Great show on Earth cannot run without patronage. We do not aspire to riches but we can show a gratifying progress." Viola Desmond died in 1965.

**STAG INN,
PRESTON, C.1890S**

There is a small hotel business that is now a big part of folklore and oral tradi-
tions in the Preston area—the famous Stag Inn. The first of its kind, it became
a landmark and a meeting and eating place in the Preston area. It was run by
William Dare until he died in the 1870s, at which point his son, George Dare,
took it over. When he died in 1895, the business was shut down.

It is understandable that there would be multiple stores in the small community of Africville—there had to be in this segregated community, which had
to rely largely on its own strengths. The Africville businesses were small, but
they were viable. Edith Macdonald Brown's grocery store was called the Handy
Store, and located at what was then 1805 Barrington Street. Her uncle opened
the store, the first in the area, in 1846. Edith Macdonald Brown ran the store
until 1952—representing more than a century of continuous family business.
Among the other prominent Africville businesses was Ida Carvery's store, called
the Penny Shop.

To count pennies in another setting, one moves on to the George Washington
Carver Credit Union. Inaugurated on July 17, 1950, it was the brain child of
three business-minded community activists in the Preston-Dartmouth area:
Councillor A. W. Evans; J. A. Ross Kinney, then superintendent of the Nova
Scotia Home for Coloured Children; and Coulter B. States, senior employee of
the Canadian National Railways.

Another initiative deserves special mention: the crafts business called Studio Wefan started by Daurene Lewis in Annapolis Royal. This was a family business in which Daurene Lewis was proprietor, designer, and weaver. She also found time to serve in municipal politics. Another successful entrepreneur, always on the move and never failing to help in the volunteer sector, is Geraldine (Clayton) Browning, one-time owner of Balloon Fantasy novelty store in Kentville. She now owns a bed and breakfast operation at her Gibson Woods home, which she calls Browning's Triple B.

From the 1980s onwards, an era of growth and modernization opened with the formation of the Black Business Consortium, spearheaded by David Hill. The time had come for the African Nova Scotian community to take its place among the more than one million small businesses operating all over Canada by 1989, at a time when some fifty black businesses were operating in the province. There was a lot of catching up to do. There was a lot going on, too, like Simmonds Paving, started by Wilfred Simmonds of North Preston in 1973. Two years later, it became the first such company in the black community to be incorporated in Nova Scotia. In addition to his business, Wilfred Simmonds held numerous volunteer positions and was a founding member of many business organizations. He died on January 5, 2005.

One leap forward was the opening of the Preston Area Business Mall in East Preston in September 1992, run by W-Five Holdings, the principals of which were Spenser Colley, president; John Ross, director; Bill Colley, secretary-treasurer; and Sinclair Williams, vice-president.

A remarkable success story in the bigger league of black business is that of Grace White, president of CanJam Trading, a food brokerage business based in Dartmouth. Grace White was recognized by the University of Toronto as the Canadian Woman Entrepreneur of the Year in 1994. She stands now in good company, for, in the words of Rustum Southwell, executive director of the Black Business Initiative, speaking in Halifax in spring 2004:

> Currently, the top three black-owned companies [in Nova Scotia] are employing more than 300 people and the top ten account for more than 430 jobs. These companies are doing around or over a million dollars in sales, with combined revenue estimated to be above $100 million. We are indeed on our way to being an influential economic class.

Getting to this point has been a long and arduous journey.

TRAVELLING PEDDLER, DARTMOUTH

When the first black immigrants arrived in Nova Scotia, access to employment was based on one's position in the pecking order of colonial society. Those at the bottom of the order could only find employment in manual labour, semi-skilled labour, dockyard labour, agricultural labour for themselves or for others, and, eventually, in the businesses they created for themselves. Had their coming and settlement been anything remotely like the organized colonization schemes that Britain promoted for white immigrants, the results for black immigrants would have been different.

But misreporting out of context and mishandling by design created impediments for black immigrants. Take, for example, the report of Nova Scotia's governor to his superior in London on October 5, 1814: "I have to state to Your Lordship that though such of them as are industrious can very well maintain themselves as a common…the generality of them are so unwilling to work that several of them are absolutely starving owing to their own idleness."

Faced with generalizations of such proportions—which take no account of recency of arrival, unfamiliarity with local conditions, absence of housing, competition from white arrivals with more desirable land grants, and other factors—blacks became stigmatized quite easily as unworthy citizens. A more encouraging view can be found in the accounts of black community members, such as this description of life in Hammonds Plains, related by elderly members of that community in 1978:

They logged and hauled their lumber to the mill to be sawn, by oxen. Later came the horse. They made barrels from fir and spruce, drums from hardwood and beech, boxes from poplar and spruce, hoops from maple and sometimes alder, sold kindling rod, and made brooms. The women made quilts, hooked mats, and knitted socks and mitts. They laboured from dawn to sunset. To carry their products to the city, they would arise at dawn and load their wagons. Most of the time they would load overnight, especially if they had a ladder wagon of barrels. It was a sight to see—a train of wagons one behind the other.

Indeed, the governor's biased remarks about African Nova Scotians being unwilling to work are roundly disproved by the multitude of examples in the historical record, of which only a few can be discussed here.

Kenneth Cromwell of Weymouth Falls was born in 1907, and went to work in the pulp mill in Weymouth at age fourteen. He moved on to the Digby Power Board, where he worked for forty years, starting in the 1930s and continuing until he retired at age sixty-five. He died on his eighty-second birthday on March 3, 1989.

Another example is of John Robert Pannill, born in Yarmouth on October 8, 1898. He served in the Merchant Marine for two years during World War I. After the war he was employed by Samuel Cunard, driving a horse-drawn coal cart to make deliveries to homes and businesses. After the Halifax Explosion, he was the only black person working for Imperial Oil, after which he worked for the Canadian Railways as a porter for forty-three years from 1918 to 1962.

Working for the railway was almost a rite of passage for black Nova Scotians.
From the 1880s to the mid-1950s they were employed as sleeping-car porters. Starting in 1926 a few were also employed in the dining car service.
Employment terms and categories were based on racial lines until 1964 when
the separate white and black unions amalgamated. Still, the colour-line mentality
prevailed for years when white train crews were unhappy to work with or under
black sleeping-car porters or dining-car stewards. Some whites were convinced
that blacks would not be able to do the job. The rise in the ranks of sleeping-car
porters of Coulter States is an example of striving to succeed. This only son of
the Rev. Wellington States and Muriel States climbed the ladder in sure steps
from sleeping-car porter to buffet porter to porter in charge to porter instructor to service instructor. Later he was assigned to special duty on three royal
trains, sometimes for a month at a time. In an interview in 1989, Coulter States
showed no bitterness or resentment: "We got along well. Blacks accepted the fact
that a place was given to them. This was our job and we did it. Later we wanted
to be waiters and conductors too. After years of negotiation, we got these jobs."

In 1953 Coulter B. States was elected president of Division 132 of the
Canadian Brotherhood of Railway Employees and Other Transport Workers.
The other officers were Eugene Williams, recording secretary; Ernest Grosse,
vice-president; T. G. McDonald, financial secretary; and Booker Roache, local
chairman. This team of pioneers featured for many decades in the many institutions and activities of the Nova Scotia black community and deserves recognition
for its pioneering contributions to societal change.

In the city of Halifax, where Wayne Adams was born, one prominent black politician associated with municipal politics is Graham Downey, whose first successful bid for a council seat was in 1974. Many tried for a council seat before and since, but he holds the record for length of service: twenty-two years on the Halifax City Council and four on the Halifax Regional Council that replaced it. Alderman Downey was deputy mayor of Halifax in 1978–79.

Black politicians have also served in municipal politics in Amherst, New Glasgow, Annapolis Royal, and Sydney. In Amherst, Councillor Donald Paris was first elected in 1976, the same year in which Councillor Francis Joseph Dorrington was elected in New Glasgow.

POLITICS

If politics is the art of becoming involved in activities to bring about change and improvements, African Nova Scotians have always been politically involved, ever since Thomas Peters took his petition to the British House of Commons in November 1790, meeting with abolitionist members of parliament and directors of the Sierra Leone Company. The complaints he filed on discriminatory practices against black immigrants led to the exodus to Sierra Leone in 1792 and to a permanent historical indictment against the white establishment. It became a legacy for generations to come. Peters was a former slave in North Carolina when he enlisted as a sergeant in a segregated black unit in the British army in 1776. He was one of sixty-seven members of this unit called Black Pioneers who came to Nova Scotia at the end of the War of Independence in 1783. Upon his arrival in Annapolis Royal on May 25, 1784, he immediately became a spokesman for blacks on the crucial and pressing issue of land grants, where promises made were not kept. Together with his fellow sergeant, Murphy Steel, he appeared at protest meetings in Nova Scotia and New Brunswick, preparing and presenting petitions to bureaucrats and Governor Parr. This was the background to his appearance in London, England, in 1790, with yet another petition.

It would be a long time before African Nova Scotians found entry into electoral politics. The first opportunities were at the grassroots level, in municipal politics. Throughout the twentieth century and beyond, black town and city councillors were elected in areas of concentrated black populations. Thomas Johnson was elected to Halifax County for the Preston area in the closing decade of the nineteenth century and served many terms until 1903. He was succeeded by John Thomas (1903–06), followed by George Diggs, who served different terms for twnety-two years (1906–28). The fourth black councillor, John Colley, served for two terms (1918–20 and 1928–31). Allan W. Evans followed with a record thirty years in office (1931–61). Evans was succeeded by William B. Thomas (1961–64) and Arnold Johnson, who served four terms (1964–76).

THE 1993 LIBERAL CABINET, INCLUDING WAYNE ADAMS

The councillor who succeeded Arnold Johnson was Patrick Lachance, a white man (1976–79). By now the demographics were changing rapidly as new settlements grew in the adjoining area of Lake Echo. The black vote could no longer be relied upon to ensure the election of a black councillor. With the election of the young and likeable Wayne Adams in 1979, a new era opened in Preston politics. He served five terms on Halifax County Council (1979–93). Following the creation in 1993 of the provincial riding of Preston, made up of a large black population, Wayne Adams was elected as the first black member of the Nova Scotia Legislative Assembly; he carried this distinction further by being appointed to Premier John Savage's cabinet. In an interview with the *Mail Star* soon after his election and appointment, Adams said that the politicians he admired were all white: John Diefenbaker, Lester Pearson, and Tommy Douglas. "There were times when I dreamed about being one of them," he said. "Yet at the same time something in the back of my head told me I could never be like them. Only white people held those jobs."

The second person to hold the Preston seat in the legislature was Yvonne Thomas Atwell, who was elected in 1998—at the time the first black woman in Atlantic Canada to hold such a seat.

DAURENE LEWIS

Daurene Lewis was first elected town councillor in Annapolis Royal in 1979. Two years later she was elected deputy mayor, and in December 1984 she was elected mayor—making her the first black mayor in Canada. She was also a descendant of another first: Rose Fortune, first black policewoman in Canada.

The first black alderman in eastern Canada was Thomas Miller, whose military service was profiled in Chapter 7. He was first elected to Sydney City Council in 1955 and went on to serve until 1972. He died on January 21, 1988. The second black alderman on the Sydney City Council was Eddie Parris, who was first elected in 1975 and served till 1988.

Born in Sydney, Calvin Ruck began his working life at the Dominion Steel and Coal Corporation in Sydney, then moved on as a sleeping-car porter with Canadian National Railways. In 1968 he began his Nova Scotia civil service career as a community development officer, followed by five years as a human rights officer. He was also a community school coordinator for four years. Like his colleagues in politics, Calvin Ruck was a long-standing member of NSAACP and served the Preston area in a number of volunteer organizations. His book on the No. 2 Construction Battalion, discussed in Chapter 7, was very well received. The recipient of numerous awards, including two honorary doctorates and the Order of Canada, Calvin Ruck was appointed to the Senate of Canada in 1998. He died in Ottawa on October 19, 2004.

CALVIN RUCK

GORDON EARLE

All three African Nova Scotian politicians who entered federal politics did so in the 1990s: one in elected office and two in appointed offices. All three had outstanding careers prior to entering politics, and all three contributed significantly to social justice issues and served in the volunteer sector with remarkable dedication. These three men are Gordon Sinclair Earle, MP; Senator Donald H. Oliver; and Senator Calvin W. Ruck.

Gordon Earle began his working life as a social welfare officer in Nova Scotia. In 1968 he joined the staff of the Nova Scotia Human Rights Commission, and four years later was appointed assistant ombudsman, a position he held until 1982, when he was appointed ombudsman for the province of Manitoba. At the time he was the youngest ombudsman in the country and the first African Canadian appointed to that office. In 1994 he returned to Nova Scotia to take up the position of deputy minister for housing and consumer affairs. Upon early retirement in 1996 he founded the Hammonds Plains Karate Club. A year later, Gordon Earle was elected Member of Parliament for Halifax West, another first in a distinguished career. Among his numerous volunteer positions, he has served as president of the Nova Scotia Association for the Advancement of Coloured People and president of the Nova Scotia Home for Coloured Children.

After a brilliant academic record at both Acadia University and Dalhousie University Law School, Donald Oliver began his working life in 1965, practising law in Halifax. While a member at Stewart McKelvey Stirling Scales, he taught at Dalhousie Law School as a part-time professor for fourteen years and also at the Technical University of Nova Scotia and Saint Mary's University. He, too, has a long list of volunteer services, which includes many of the organizations mentioned in earlier pages, including founding president of the Black Cultural Society, founding director of the Black United Front, vice-president of the NSAACP, and life director of the Neptune Theatre Foundation. Donald Oliver was appointed to the Senate of Canada on September 7, 1990.

The public-spirited organizations and individuals engaged in volunteer activism have made an invaluable contribution to society: turning challenges into opportunities without much fuss and fanfare, but with effective results.

FIRST CONGRESS OF COLORED WOMEN, HALIFAX, 1920

The Ladies Auxiliary of the AUBA was one such body. It was inaugurated in East Preston on September 3, 1917, under its first president, Maude Sparks. Two of the other founding members of the Ladies Auxiliary, Sara Middleton and Edith Samuels Sparks, came from the Dartmouth community. Known popularly as the Meeting of Women at the Well—after the locale of their first meeting—women led the way to buttress the work of the AUBA which, like most organizations of the time, was male dominated. Men followed decades later when the Laymen's Council was formed in 1944.

The work of the women was so successful that in 1918 the annual convention of the AUBA resolved that where possible every affiliated church should have a ladies auxiliary. To carry this out, a full-time salaried organizer, Margaret Upshaw, was appointed; she held the position until her death in 1922. Funds were collected and the groundwork was laid for the First Congress of Colored Women, held in Halifax in 1920. The Ladies Auxiliary of the AUBA had earned national recognition in the short time of three years.

The presidents of the Ladies Auxiliary from 1917 to 1953 were Maude Sparks (1917–19), Bessie Wyse (1919–20), Muriel States (1920–21), Louisa Bundy (1921–28), Edith Samuels (Sparks) (1928–34), Izie Dora White (1934–42), and Gertrude Smith (1942–53).

Since the birth of the ladies auxiliary coincided with plans for the building of the Nova Scotia Home for Coloured Children, women were a strong force in collecting funds and supporting the project. In later years many prominent women supported the ladies auxiliary as well as the Women's Missionary Society. Among them were Muriel States, Edith Cromwell, Pearleen Oliver, Ruth Johnson, Alfaretta Anderson, and Daisy Fairfax. The pioneering work of these trailblazers surely brightened the path for others to follow.

In the African Nova Scotian communities throughout the province, volunteerism, whether in the communities or in society at large has been a constant characteristic. From the early times when survival and self-help were two sides of the coin, this characteristic has survived over the ages. To tell this story in full would require a special study. In this volume, the authors wish to pay tribute to the thousands of volunteers over more than three hundred years—some already mentioned and many not mentioned—by selecting two further examples from two generations: both physically towering personalities, both charismatic in different ways, both articulate, fearless, dedicated, and rising to the challenges of their day. The older man is Winston Spenser Ruck. Born in 1923, he died on August 15, 1992, in Sydney. The second is Burnley Allen "Rocky" Jones, born in Truro in 1941, and mentioned already in Chapters 5 and 6. The former was acknowledged as the "diplomat"; the latter, however he earned the popular accolade of "Rocky," never hesitated to rock the boat when it served to advance the cause of social justice.

WINSTON RUCK

Winston Ruck began working in the Sydney Steel Plant in 1940 at the age of seventeen. Thirty years later, he was elected president of the United Steel Workers of America, Local 1064, the first and only black person to hold that office. He served in the Royal Canadian Air Force in World War II. Years later, in 1986, he was awarded life membership in the Royal Canadian Legion, Branch 128. He served on numerous boards, including those of the Black United Front, the Black Cultural Centre, the Nova Scotia Rehabilitation Centre, and Enterprise Cape Breton. He took over as interim executive director of the BUF in 1989, a particularly difficult time, and served it well. For his volunteer services he received the Tom Miller Humanitarian Award, and his hometown of

Syndey conferred on him the honour of honorary citizen. His philosophy—as he explained it to the *Mail Star* in 1992—was far-reaching:

> *Those in authority have to reach out to all minorities and bring them into the fold. There must be the political will. We're all brothers and sisters, we have more in common than not in common. Our differences are small.*

Also in 1992, the *Cape Breton Magazine* conducted an exhaustive interview with Winston Ruck, two months before he died. It is a remarkable interview, in which he spoke of the human condition in trying times without bitterness and with candour and class.

Four years before the appearance of that interview, George Elliott Clarke wrote a column in the *Daily News* (April 9, 1988), whose opening paragraph read: "Burnley (Rocky) Jones is a prophet without honour in his own land." Clarke went on to refer to the two sides of Jones' considerable repertoire. The one side: "In those turbulent days [i.e., the 1960s], Jones, a populist bohemian, was in the thick of every crisis, attending teach-ins, drop-ins and sit-ins, spinning James Brown records and talking Marxism." The other side: "Yet because he was able to negotiate in boardrooms as effectively as he could orate in the streets, Jones achieved several constructive changes."

Jones joined the Canadian Armed Forces in Vancouver soon after leaving school, and not long afterwards was drawn into the Students Union for Peace Action in Toronto—his initiation into political struggle. A branch was formed in Halifax at Kwacha House, where youth converged to tackle issues of racism and poverty. Other areas of national and local involvement followed for Jones, such as the Afro–Canadian Liberation Movement, the National Black Coalition of Canada, and the Black United Front. One of the founders of Dalhousie's Transition Year Programme for students from Black and Mi'kmaq communities as well as the later Indigenous Black and Mi'kmaq Programme at the Dalhousie Law School, Burnley Jones led by example, moving his own education upwards, from the grade-nine he had when he left school to university degrees to joining the legal profession. On June 16, 2004, he was awarded the honorary degree of Doctor of Laws by the University of Guelph. Jones was no longer the prophet without honour but the once and future champion of the never-ending struggle to sustain a just society for all.

Africville:
A Lingering Legacy of Mixed Messages

AFRICVILLE SCHOOLCHILDREN, C.1940S

Africville was a black settlement that originally comprised fifteen acres of land in Division K of Halifax. It was made up of three lots of five acres each. From its original size of fifteen acres, Division K expanded to eighty acres (sixteen lots of five acres). This division was first owned by whites. Some time between 1815 and 1848 black immigrants moved in from the Preston and Hammonds Plains areas, and perhaps from other areas in close vicinity. In 1848 two black residents, William Brown and William Arnold, obtained title deeds to plots of land in Division K. The list grew to include others, giving rise to the following family list of original owners of land in Division

K: Brown, Carvery, Dixon, Arnold, Hill, Fletcher, Bailey, Grant, and Roans. With the organization of a church in 1849, the Africville saga was launched on its long and uneven course until it gave way, involuntarily and painfully, to Seaview Park, which was officially opened on June 23, 1985. The saga did not, however, end in 1985; it continued with the formation of the Africville Genealogy Society and its advocacy of just compensation for the displacement. This society was founded in September 1982 by three members: Brenda Steed Ross, Debra Dixon Jones, and Linda Mantley. Others joined later.

ROCKHEAD PRISON

Africville started off as a promising rural settlement, but within a few decades it was challenged by the forces of industrialization, as the population of Halifax grew from 21,000 to 47,000 between 1851 and 1911. New industries chose sites near the shores of the Bedford Basin close to Africville: an oil plant storage facility, a bonemill fertilizer factory, a cotton mill, two slaughter houses, a tar factory, and leather-tanning and stone-crushing industries. Rockhead Prison was also built less than a hundred metres away. What followed was worse: night soil disposal pits, an infectious diseases hospital, and a city garbage dump. Surrounded by factory and filth, it was denied electricity, pipe-borne water, police protection, and every city amenity, even though it was within city boundaries and inhabited by city residents and taxpayers.

In 1945 Halifax City Council began talking about relocating Africville and in 1961 they decided to demolish it, in spite of the protests of many residents. Africville had been a settlement of gardens and stores, animals and poultry, a post office, a school, a church, and residents with pride in their heritage and their possessions, beleaguered and neglected as they were. Within the short space of a decade (1960–70) it was all over: the residents were relocated, many of them into public housing; a new bridge would be built, and, in time, a park and a container terminal would replace the historic community. But issues of fair compensation and justice for the former residents and their descendants lived on in literature and debates, in exhibitions, and even in the forums of the United Nations.

Since the appearance of the article in the *Star Weekly* on January 1, 1966, bearing the cover caption "Africville: A Proud People Fight for their Homes in Halifax's Negro Ghetto," countless books and articles, videos and interviews, speeches, conferences, and exhibitions have appeared, pioneered by Donald H. Clairmont and Dennis William Magill in *Africville: The Life and Death of a Canadian Black Community*. Some later additions include *The Spirit of Africville*, selected and edited by the Africville Genealogy Society (with contributions by Donald Clairmont, Stephen Kimber, Bridglal Pachai, and Charles Saunders), and *Africville: A Spirit that Lives On*, with contributions by Charles Saunders, Bridglal Pachai, and Donald Clairmont.

In 1987 the president of the Africville Genealogy Society, Brenda Steed Ross, wrote, "My opinion is, if we had remained in Africville, and given the adequate assistance needed such as water and sewage, paved roads, recreational facilities, also assistance in maintaining our properties, we would still be functioning as a community today." This was reiterated at a workshop convened by the Black Cultural Centre at the North Branch Public Library on Gottingen Street in Halifax, on September 13, 1986. Oral testimonies were given by older residents who spoke of growing up in Africville: Matilda Newman, Eletha Manley, Elsie Desmond, Jessica Kane, Ruth Johnson, Laura Howe, Wilhemina Byers, and Mrs. Roland Howe. Individually, collectively, and spontaneously, these residents spoke of communal bonds, of religious bonds, of mutual self-help; of their well-kept homes and gardens; of their homecrafts and their strength in music; of their church and school; and of their pastors, deacons, teachers and elders. Their hearts and minds spoke of a loving and much-loved Africville—far from the negative generalizations of those who looked at Africville from the outside with a jaundiced vision.

The images of Africville in this volume speak to the ravages caused by the city's neglect of an area less than ten kilometres from city hall, of a lively community contributing to city life and city institutions. The unfavourable spotlight on city politics and policies caused the city council to move when, perhaps, it was too late to remedy decades of blatant neglect. While the past cannot be restored, the future can be well used to redress whatever perceived or real injustices exist. That is the hope with which 2005 opened as all levels of government—municipal, provincial, and federal—became engaged in discussions to review the ongoing demands of the Africville Genealogy Society. The society's case for proper compensation included a building to memorialize the former Africville Church and the construction of apartment buildings for former residents and their descendants. Its presentations were also made to the United Nations conference on racism, racial discrimination, xenophobia, and related intolerance in Durban, South Africa, in 2001. Three years later, a United Nations report called for compensation to redress the historical injustice. Along the way, the Department of Canadian Heritage designated Africville a national historic site in 2002.

Select Bibliography

Annual Minutes of the African United Baptist Association, 1984–1987.

Beaton-Planetta, Elizabeth. "A Tale of Three Churches: Ethnic Architecture in Sydney, Nova Scotia." *Canadian Ethnic Studies* vol. 16, no. 3 (1984): 89–110.

Bertley, Leo W. *Canada and Its People of African Descent.* Bilongo Publishers, 1977.

Best, Carrie M. *That Lonesome Road: The Autobiography of Carrie M. Best.* Clarion Publishing, 1977.

McKerrow, P. E.. *A Brief History of Blacks in Nova Scotia (1783–1895).* Edited and introduced by Frank Stanley Boyd Jr. Afro–Nova Scotian Enterprises, 1975. (Originally published 1895.)

Clayton, Willard Parker. *Whatever Your Will Lord: Emmanual Baptist Church, Upper Hammonds Plains, Nova Scotia, 1845–1984.* Lancelot Press, 1984.

Davidson, Stephen Eric. "Leaders of Black Baptists of Nova Scotia, 1782–1832." BA honours thesis. Acadia University, April 1975.

Evans, Doris, and Gertrude Tynes. *Telling the Truth, Reflections: Segregated Schools in Nova Scotia.* Lancelot Press, 1995.

Fosty, George and Darril. *Black Ice: The Lost History of the Colored Hockey League of the Maritimes, 1895–1925.* Stryker-Indigo Publishing Company, 2004.

Gordon, Grant. *From Slavery to Freedom: The Life of David George, Pioneer Black Baptist Minister.* Lancelot Press, 1992.

Grant, John N. *The Immigration and Settlement of the Black Refugees of the War of 1812 in Nova Scotia and New Brunswick.* Black Cultural Centre for Nova Scotia, 1990.

_____. *The Maroons in Nova Scotia.* Formac Publishing, 2002.

Head, Wilson, *A Life on the Edge: Experiences in "Black and White" in North America.* University of Toronto Press, 1995.

Johnston, A. J. B. "Mathieu DaCosta and Early Canada: Possibilities and Probabilities." Parks Canada, n.d.

Johnston, Marcus Justin. *James Robinson Johnston: The Life, Death, and Legacy of Nova Scotia's First Black Lawyer.* Nimbus Publishing, 2005.

Kyte, Jack, et al. *Native Born: A Brief History of the Black Presence in Pictou County.* Scott Maritimes, 1990.

Oliver, Pearleen. "A Root and a Name." Rev. Richard Preston, 1975.

_____. "From Generation to Generation: Bi-Centennial of the Black Church in Nova Scotia, 1785–1985." Black Cultural Centre for Nova Scotia, 1985.

_____. *Song of the Spirit: An Historical Narrative on the History of the Beechville United Baptist Church, 150th Anniversary, 1844–1994.* Lancelot Press, 1994.

Pachai, Bridglal. *Beneath the Clouds of the Promised Land: The Survival of Nova Scotia's Blacks.* 2 vols. Black Educators Association, 1987–89.

_____. *William Hall: Winner of the Victoria Cross.* Four East Publications, 1995.

Paris, Cherry M., ed. *A Brief History of Acaciaville United Baptist Church.* Acaciaville United Baptist Church, 1993.

Paris, Peter J. "The Moral, Political and Religious Significance of the Black Churches in Nova Scotia." Black Cultural Centre for Nova Scotia, 1989.

Robinson, Carey. *The Fighting Maroons of Jamaica.* William Collins and Sangster, 1969.

Saunders, Charles R.. *Share and Care: The Story of the Nova Scotia Home for Colored Children.* Nimbus Publishing, 1994.

_____. *Sweat and Soul: The Saga of Black Boxers from the Halifax Forum to Caesar's Palace.* Lancelot Press, 1990.

Thomas, Carolyn G., ed. *Reflections: The East Preston United Baptist Church on its 150th Anniversary.* East Preston United Baptist Church, 1996.

Walker, James W. St. G. *A History of Blacks in Canada: A Study Guide for Teachers and Students.* Supply and Services Canada, 1980.

Whitney Pier Student Project, Black Cultural Centre.

Williams, Dawn P. *Who's Who in Black Canada.* Williams and Associates, 2002.

Williams, Savanah E. "The Role of the African United Baptist Association in the Development of Indigenous African Canadians in Nova Scotia, 1782–1978" (privately held).

Wilson, Ellen Gibson. *The Loyal Blacks.* Capricorn Books, 1976.

Winks, Robin W. *The Blacks in Canada: A History.* McGill-Queens University Press, 1971.

Image Sources

A Brief History of the Coloured Baptists of Nova Scotia: 60

Black Cultural Centre: cover, 2, 5, 9, 13, 14, 16, 17, 22, 24, 25, 26, 27, 31, 37, 47, 51, 53, 56, 58 (bottom left), 67t, 76, 78, 83, 84, 86, 88, 89, 91, 92, 98, 99, 100, 102, 103, 104, 105, 108, 110, 111, 113, 114, 118, 121, 123, 125

Black Loyalist Heritage Society: 12

Wayne Adams 19, 97; Henry Bishop 20; Walter Borden 106; Geraldine Browning 94, 112; Irvine Carvery 126; Gerald Clarke 81, Ken Crawford 58 (top left); Jarvis Darville 39, 40; Jack Desmond 75; Graham Downey 116; Gordon Earle 119; Fairfax Family 38; Mayann Francis 29; Edith Gray 59, 67 (bottom), 68, 69, 90, 96; Robert Maxwell 95; Winifred Milne and Sylvia Bell 70, 72; Bridglal Pachai 55, 57, 58 (top right), 77; Geeta Paray-Clarke 107; Sherrolynn Riley 33; Arthur Ruck 50; Lisellote Sawh 124; Coulter States 115; Vincent Waterman 30; Lorne White 34, 35; Eugene Williams 74; Michelle Williams 55, 58 (bottom right)

Nova Scotia Advisory Council on the Status of Women: 120

Nova Scotia Archives and Records Management: 43, 44 (left), 45, 88

Nova Scotia Museum: 36

Province of Nova Scotia: 66, 117

Queen's University Archives: 44 (right)

Toronto Star (Feb. 18, 1996): 79

Images of our Past

Uncovering the rich history of the Maritimes, one community at a time. Check out these and other *Images of Our Past* titles at your local bookstore or online at www.nimbus.ns.ca

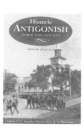

Historic Shelburne

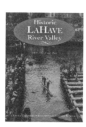

Historic Guysborough

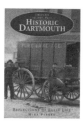

Historic Dartmouth

Historic North End Halifax

Historic LaHave River Valley

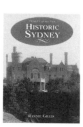

Historic Sydney

Historic Antigonish

Historic Kentville

Historic Colchester